over the top...
...and on the side

over the top...
and on the side

Silvana Franco and Shirley Gill

LORENZ BOOKS
NEW YORK • LONDON • SYDNEY • BATH

This edition published in 1997 by Lorenz Books

This edition published in the USA by Lorenz Books
27 West 20th Street
New York
NY 10011

LORENZ BOOKS are available for bulk purchase
for sales promotion and for premium use. For details write or call
the manager of special sales: Lorenz Books,
27 West 20th Street, New York, NY 10011. (212) 807-6739

ISBN 1 85967 485 2

Publisher: Joanna Lorenz
Senior Cookery Editor: Linda Fraser
Assistant Editor: Margaret Malone
Designers: Kim Bale, Visual Image and Brian Weldon
Photographers: William Adams-Lingwood, Edward Allwright and James Duncan
Home Economists: Lucy McKelvie, Jenny Shapter and Elizabeth Silver
Additional Recipes: Maxine Clark, Jenny Stacey and Steven Wheeler

Printed and bound in Hong Kong

1 3 5 7 9 10 8 6 4 2

CONTENTS

Introduction	6
Techniques	18
CLASSIC SAUCES	25
SAUCES *for* MEAT *and* POULTRY	48
SAUCES *for* FISH *and* SEAFOOD	56
SAUCES *for* PASTA *and* VEGETABLES	64
MARINADES	74
SALSAS	88
RELISHES *and* RAITAS	126
DIPS *and* DRESSINGS	138
SAUCES *for* DESSERTS	168
Index	190

INTRODUCTION

Light or creamy, rich or tangy, fiery or mild, a sauce, salsa, relish or marinade will transform any dish from the entirely ordinary to the simply divine. Choosing the correct sauce is all important – it should enhance the dish it is served with and not overpower it. The simple classic sauces are easy to select since they're traditionally served with foods that they go particularly well with: mint sauce with lamb, apple sauce with pork, or cranberry with turkey, for instance.

The more complicated classic sauces can generally be served with a broader range of dishes and you'll find that the recipes in this section often have several serving suggestions. The three chapters that follow provide a selection of sauces for meat, poultry, fish, seafood, pasta and vegetables.

A sauce isn't always added after cooking – it may also be an essential part of a dish, like those in the marinade chapter. In these the flavors blend so well, that you are hardly aware of the sauce at all.

Salsas, which are fresh, uncooked sauces, have become very fashionable. Simple to prepare and very versatile, these flavorful mixtures can be served either as a dip or as a sauce. They can be fruity, spicy hot or creamy and are delicious with all sorts of foods from tortilla chips and crudités to broiled chicken and fish.

The final two savory chapters include a wide range of tart and tangy relishes, cool creamy yogurt raitas, delicious dips and a selection of dressings for salads.

Sauces, of course, aren't always savory and the last chapter provides a delectable selection of sweet sauces to serve with desserts. There are creamy sauces and custards to serve with fruit pies and crumbles, tart fruit sauces, a rich fudgy chocolate sauce and fresh and fruity salsas to serve with ice creams.

The introduction is full of information on ingredients and there are professional cook's tips on classic and contemporary sauce-making techniques. So, whether you are an experienced cook, or never previously ventured further than the ketchup bottle, *over the top... and on the side* will provide inspiration to liven up your meals.

Fruit

The varying colors, flavors and textures of fruits make them the ideal ingredient for many salsas, relishes and dips.

Bananas
Packed with nutrients and full of flavor, bananas are worth buying when they are at their best. Choose a bunch that is deep yellow, firm to the touch and without black spots on them.

Melons
There are lots of different melons available depending upon the time of year. Crisp-fleshed watermelons and juicy, orange-fleshed melons, such as cantaloupe, make great fruity salsas.

Papayas
Also known as pawpaw, the papaya is a sweet-fleshed fruit with edible seeds. It is rich in vitamin A and acts as a very good digestive aid when served at the end of a meal.

Pineapples
Pineapple can be used in both sweet and savory dishes but must be served when ripe and fresh. Choose fruit that feels firm, with a definite pineapple aroma; a leaf pulled from the center should come out easily.

Passion fruit
Cut the fruit in half to reveal the succulent, aromatic pulp and edible seeds. Serve with other tropical fruit or with ice cream.

Mangoes
Mango is wonderful for serving fresh in salsas and dips or cooking down into sweet chutney. The ripeness of mango is not determined by color: to test the fruit, press it gently. The flesh should give slightly when ripe.

Oranges
The juice, flesh and grated rind of oranges are both fragrant and flavorful. Use them to add a delicious tangy sparkle to sauces, relishes and fruity salsas.

Vegetables

From sweet, versatile corn to zesty, pungent onions, vegetables make an ideal base for – or a colorful crunchy addition to – all sorts of salsas, relishes and dips.

Avocados
The skin and large pit of the avocado are inedible. The flesh, however, can be mashed until smooth and creamy to make a perfect salsa base. Avocado discolors quickly, so brush cut surfaces with lemon juice to preserve them, and use any avocado-based salsa soon after mixing.

Cucumbers
Cool refreshing cucumbers chosen for salsas and crudités must feel firm to the touch. The skin adds texture and fiber, so avoid peeling them.

Onions
Scallions, red onions, shallots and everyday onions are all frequently used in salsas, relishes and dips. Scallions and red onions are mild enough to serve raw, while shallots and ordinary onions melt into sweetness when cooked gently over low heat.

Peppers
Red, yellow and orange bell peppers have a sweet flavor that is enhanced by roasting and grilling. Green peppers taste fresh and herby and are best sliced or served raw in salads or salsas.

Corn
If buying fresh corn, choose plump ears with tightly packed kernels. Remove the papery leaves and silks, or husk, and boil in plain water (salt toughens the kernels) for 5 minutes, until bright yellow. Lift out of the water, season with salt and smother with butter.

Tomatoes
The most essential salsa ingredient – opt for plump, firm-fleshed tomatoes that are a deep shade of red. Though available all year, tomatoes are at their best in summer, simply because they are often grown in hot-houses during winter months and are then not only expensive but also lacking in flavor.

Spices and Flavorings

Whereas herbs are generally the leaf parts of a plant, spices may be made from the seeds, bark, stems or roots. They are usually dried and may be sold whole or ground. As with herbs, keep them in airtight jars in a dark cupboard, especially ground spices which loose their flavor more quickly than their whole counterparts. For the fullest flavor buy in small quantities and use up quickly.

Capers
These give a piquant note and are especially good with fish.

Cardamoms
These oval, light green pods are very aromatic. They can be used whole or the seeds removed and crushed for a warm spicy flavor.

Chilies and Cayenne
Fresh and dried chilies add heat and vary according to size and color. Generally, but not always, large, pale green chilies will be milder than small red ones. Dried chilies are always hotter than fresh. Cayenne is a very hot chili. Wash your hands thoroughly after preparing chilies and if possible wear thin rubber gloves.

Cinnamon sticks
This is the sweetly flavored rolled bark of a tropical evergreen tree. It can be bought ground, but the sticks give a mellow flavor to syrups and are easily removed.

Cloves
The plump, dried flower buds from an evergreen tree. They are aromatic with a faint bitter taste.

Coriander seeds
A sweet, warm, aromatic spice, also available ground.

Garlic
A strongly flavored member of the onion family, and should therefore be used in moderation. For less a pungent flavor, increase the cooking time. The pinky-purple cloves are considered to have a better flavor than the white varieties.

Ginger, fresh and dried
Fresh gingerroot is the plump bulbous rhizome of the ginger plant. It is knobbly and should be peeled thinly with a potato peeler or sharp knife and chopped or grated. It has a hot, sharp, fresh taste quite different from ground ginger which is hot and peppery.

Juniper berries
These small purply-black berries have a sweet resinous aroma which can be released by crushing with a heavy-bladed knife before use.

Lemon grass
The bulbous base of this lemon-scented grass is usually used. It can be crushed and used whole or chopped for a stronger flavor.

Mace
This is the thin lacy cover of the nutmeg seed and has a similar, though more gentle, flavor. It is sold ground although whole mace is sometimes available.

Mustard
Comes as brown, black or white seed as well as traditional mustard powder, ground mustard seed blended with turmeric. It is a great flavor enhancer for cheese and egg sauces but should be used in moderation as it can be hot.

Nutmeg
Is the ripened dried seed of a large tropical tree. It has a rich mellow flavor which is greatly enhanced if freshly grated.

Paprika
A sweet, piquant spice, ideal for enhancing the flavor of vegetables and meat.

Peppercorns
Pepper is a universal seasoning. Dried black and white peppercorns are best freshly ground for the most pungency. Green peppercorns are available fresh, bottled in brine or dried.

Saffron
This is the dried thread-like stigma of a crocus. It gives a rich golden yellow color and slightly musty sweet flavor to sauces.

Shallots
These are another member of the onion family and have a strong but more mellow flavor than the ordinary onion.

Turmeric
Like saffron, turmeric also gives a rich yellow color to any sauce. Use in moderation as too much will leave an acrid bitter taste.

Vanilla pod
Used whole for a rich flavor.

nutmeg

green cardamoms

cayenne

juniper berries

fresh
gingerroot

mace

saffron

dried ginger

chili

turmeric

coriander
seeds

shallots

cloves

capers

green chili

red chilies

mustard

lemon grass

black
peppercorns

paprika

cinnamon
sticks

green peppercorns

vanilla pod

garlic

Herbs

Herbs are simply edible plants whose leaves have a particularly strong flavor or aroma when they are crushed or heated. It is usual to use just the leaves stripped from coarse stalks, but occasionally softer stalks and flowers are used too.

By far the best way to use herbs is straight from the garden. You'll find they can be grown in a comparatively small area and given a sunny position most will thrive on poor soils or, failing that, pot a few and stand on a brightly lit window-sill. Supermarkets now offer an increasing selection of pot-grown or prepacked fresh herbs. These are fine, especially out of season when there is little available from the garden; however, they can be soft and do not have the robust flavor of a freshly-picked garden crop.

Dried herbs are also useful in winter but a number lose their flavor and acquire hay-like overtones during drying and storage. Choose freeze-dried brands for the best flavor and store in airtight containers in a dark cupboard. Glass jars on a brightly lit spice rack may look attractive but are not ideal for the purpose.

Bay
Has dark green, leathery leaves which are generally used whole to impart a delicate flavor to sauces. To increase the flavor crush the leaf in your hand or tear into pieces. It is an essential component of a bouquet garni.

Chervil
A very delicate herb with soft, lacy, fern-like leaves. It has a very mild anise flavor so use plenty of it and only add near the end of cooking.

Chives
These have slender, cylindrical, grass-like leaves with a mild onion flavor. Use fresh with egg and cheese dishes.

Cilantro
Cilantro, with its finely scalloped broad leaf, has a spicy flavor. Leaves and stalks can be used, particularly fresh in salsas. It is essential in Indian dishes.

Dill
A distinctive, pungent herb with blue-green feathery leaves. It goes well with fish and egg dishes and also cream sauces.

Mint
Well known for its freshly flavored, bright green leaves. Traditionally used with lamb, it is also good with fish and some vegetable dishes.

Oregano and marjoram
These herbs are from the same family. They both have small, oval, peppery-flavored leaves which enhance tomato-based sauces. Oregano has a more robust flavor than sweeter marjoram.

Parsley
Two varieties of this widely-used herb are available, curly parsley and italian parsley. Italian parsley has a more concentrated flavor but curly parsley is more easily chopped. If using parsley in a marinade, stock or bouquet garni, use most of the stalk as this has a more concentrated flavor.

Rosemary
Rosemary has aromatic needle-like leaves. They are coarse and pungent so use sparingly and chop very finely.

Tarragon
With its long, narrow, glossy leaves and warm, anise flavor, tarragon is an essential sauce flavoring. Use fresh French tarragon rather than Russian or dried tarragon.

Thyme
This herb has tiny oval leaves with a strong flavor and goes well with most dishes. Some varieties have a lemon scent which goes well with chicken and fish dishes. It is coarse, so remove the leaves from the stalks.

italian parsley

tarragon

parsley

chives

dill

chervil

mint

cilantro

thyme

rosemary

oregano

bay

marjoram

Instant Dips

Whip up some speedy dips for an impromptu cocktail party or to impress unexpected guests with the help of prepared classics, such as mayonnaise, sun-dried tomatoes and soy sauce.

Creamy black olive dip

To make a great dip for bread sticks, stir a little black olive paste into a carton of sour cream until smooth and well blended. Add salt and freshly ground black pepper and a squeeze of fresh lemon juice to taste. Serve chilled. For a low-calorie version, substitute low-fat or plain yogurt for the sour cream.

Crème fraîche or sour cream with scallions

Finely chop a bunch of scallions and stir into a carton of crème fraîche or sour cream. Add a dash of chili sauce, a squeeze of fresh lime juice and a little salt and freshly ground black pepper to taste. Serve with tortilla chips or alongside a spicy guacamole.

Yogurt and mustard dip

Mix a small carton of creamy plain yogurt with one or two tsp of wholegrain mustard. Serve with grissini or crudités.

Herbed mayonnaise

Liven up ready-made French-style mayonnaise with a handful of chopped fresh herbs – try Italian parsley, basil, dill or tarragon. Season to taste with plenty of freshly ground black pepper and serve with crisp carrot and cucumber batons.

Passata and horseradish dip

Bring a little tang to a small carton or bottle of passata (sieved tomatoes) by adding some horseradish sauce or a tsp or two of ground horseradish. Add salt and pepper to taste and serve with spicy tortilla chips.

Pesto dip

For a simple, speedy Italian-style dip, stir a tbsp of ready-made red or green pesto into a carton of sour cream. Serve with crisp crudités or wedges of oven-roasted Mediterranean vegetables, such as peppers, zucchini and onions.

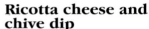

Ricotta cheese and chive dip

Mix a tub of skim milk ricotta cheese with two or three tbsp of chopped fresh chives, and season to taste with salt and plenty of black pepper. If the dip is a little too thick, stir in a spoonful or two of milk to soften it.

Yogurt and sun-dried tomato dip

Stir one or two tbsp of finely chopped sun-dried tomatoes into a carton of plain yogurt. Season to taste with salt and freshly ground black pepper. Serve with small triangles of crisp toasted pita bread or crackers. Alternatively, use sour cream in place of the yogurt.

Spiced yogurt dip

To make a speedy Indian-style dip, stir a little mild or hot and spicy curry paste into a carton of plain yogurt. Add a finely chopped apple or a spoonful or two of mango chutney and serve with crisp poppadums.

Creamy black
olive dip

Crème fraîche with
scallions

Yogurt and
sun-dried tomato dip

Herbed
mayonnaise

Yogurt and mustard
dip

Ricotta
cheese
and chive
dip

Spiced yogurt dip

Pesto dip

Passata and
horseradish dip

Serving Suggestions

There are many ways to serve salsas, relishes and dips: they can be spooned on the side or over the top of fish, chicken or meat dishes, used as a sandwich filling or topping, or served with antipasti or cheese. One fun way to serve them is with a selection of foods for dipping.

Bread sticks
Choose crunchy Italian-style grissini bread sticks for thick and creamy dips and salsas. To serve them, either pile the bread sticks on a plate or in a large bowl, or stand them in a tall glass or pitcher.

Cheese straws
These are ideal for dipping and dunking. You can buy cheese straws ready-made, but they are very easy to make at home. Simply roll out a small package of puff pastry thinly and cut it into strips. Lightly brush the strips with beaten egg and sprinkle with a little grated cheese. (Twist the strips first, if desired.) Chill for 10 minutes, then bake them at 350°F for 15–20 minutes or until puffed and golden. Cool on a wire rack before serving.

Corn chips
These crisp ready-made Mexican-style snacks are now widely available in delicatessens and supermarkets. Choose cheese-flavored corn chips for creamy dips and the plain variety for spicier tomato-based salsas. Look out for tasty blue corn chips in specialty shops and food halls.

Fruit crudités
These make the perfect accompaniment to sweet dips. Cut chunks of peach, nectarine, pear, banana or apple and arrange on a platter with whole or halved strawberries, segments of oranges, plums, and not-too-ripe figs.

Potato chips
Salted chips, either the plain variety or one of the many flavored, are a popular standby and make a great accompaniment to absolutely any dip. Choose the thicker ones for chunky or very thick dips and only serve light, creamy dips with the more fragile varieties.

Tortilla chips
The classic accompaniment to chilled tomato salsa, tortilla chips are now available in a variety of flavors. Serve the fiery chips with creamy dips and the cool ones with robust salsas or relishes.

Vegetable chips
There are some brands of vegetable chips available ready-made, but they are also easy to make at home. Several different vegetables work well, try sweet potato, beet, carrot, parsnip or, of course, potato. Peel the vegetables, slice them wafer-thin with a mandoline or swivel-style vegetable peeler, then deep-fry the slices in hot vegetable oil and season them with plenty of salt and a little chili powder, paprika or cayenne pepper.

Vegetable crudités
Chunks, sticks or wedges of fresh raw vegetables make perfect scoops for all kinds of dips and salsas. Try carrot, celery and cucumber sticks; cut thin strips of more than one color of bell pepper; or trim small florets of cauliflower or broccoli. To make wedges or "scoops," cut small peppers lengthwise into thin wedges, trim celery into short lengths, or cut 2-in pieces of cucumber into sixths lengthwise and remove the seeds. Crisp endive leaves and the small interior leaves of Romaine or Boston lettuces also make delicious crudités.

Bread sticks and
cheese straws

Fruit
crudités

Vegetable
crudités

Corn chips

Tortilla chips

Vegetable chips

Potato chips

TECHNIQUES

Stocks

Many sauces depend for their depth and richness on a good quality stock base. Fresh stock will give the most balanced flavor and it is worth the effort to make it at home. It may be frozen successfully for several months. Canned beef bouillon and chicken broth are good substitutes. For everyday cooking, most cooks will use stock cubes, but these often have a salt base so taste carefully and season lightly.

FISH STOCK

INGREDIENTS
any fish bones, skin and
   trimmings available
1 onion
1 carrot
1 celery stalk
6 black peppercorns
2 bay leaves
3 stalks parsley

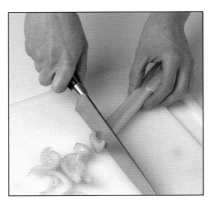

1 Peel and coarsely slice the onion. Peel and chop the carrot, and scrub and slice the celery.

2 Place all the ingredients in a large saucepan and add enough water to cover. Bring to a boil, skim the surface and simmer uncovered for 20 minutes.

3 Strain and use immediately or store for two days in the refrigerator.

BROWN STOCK

INGREDIENTS
2 tbsp vegetable oil
3 lb shin, shank or neck of beef
   bones, cut into pieces
8 oz shin of beef, cut into pieces
bouquet garni
2 onions, trimmed and quartered
2 carrots, scrubbed and chopped
2 celery sticks, sliced
1 tsp black peppercorns
1/2 tsp salt

1 Drizzle the vegetable oil over the bottom of a roasting pan, add the bones and meat. Coat in oil and bake at 425°F for 25–30 minutes or until well browned, turning regularly during cooking.

2 Transfer the meat and bones to a large saucepan, add the remaining ingredients and cover with 14 cups of water. Bring to the boil, skim the surface, then partially cover and simmer for 2 1/2–3 hours or until reduced to 7 cups.

3 Strain the stock into a bowl. Cool and remove the solidified fat before use. Store for up to 4 days in the refrigerator.

CHICKEN OR WHITE STOCK

INGREDIENTS
1 onion
4 cloves
1 carrot
2 leeks
2 celery stalks
1 chicken carcass, cooked or raw,
  or 1¹/₂ lb veal bones cut into
  pieces
bouquet garni
8 black peppercorns
¹/₂ tsp salt

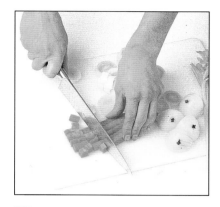

1 Peel the onion, cut into quarters and spike each quarter with a clove. Scrub and coarsely chop the vegetables.

2 Break up the chicken carcass and place in a large saucepan with the remaining ingredients.

3 Cover with 7 cups water. Bring to a boil, skim the surface and simmer, partially covered, for 2 hours. Strain the stock into a bowl and allow to cool. When cold remove the hardened fat before using. Store for up to 4 days in the refrigerator.

VEGETABLE STOCK

INGREDIENTS
2 tbsp vegetable oil
1 onion
2 carrots
2 large celery stalks, plus any
  small amounts from the
  following: leeks, celery root,
  parsnip, turnip, cabbage or
  cauliflower trimmings,
  mushrooms peelings
bouquet garni
6 black peppercorns

1 Peel, halve and slice the onion. Coarsely chop the remaining vegetables.

2 Heat the oil in a large pan and sauté the onion and vegetables until soft and lightly browned. Add the remaining ingredients and cover with 7 cups water.

3 Bring to a boil, skim the surface, then partially cover and simmer for 1¹/₂ hours. Strain the stock and allow to cool. Store in the refrigerator for 2–3 days.

Thickening a Sauce

The simplest way to turn a liquid into a richer, more delicious sauce is to reduce it by bringing to a rolling boil over a high heat. However, there are many other methods, depending on the ingredients used in the dish you are cooking.

ROUX BASES

A roux, flour cooked gently in butter or oil, is the most common method of thickening. Generally equal quantities of butter and flour are used and the length of cooking time determines the type of sauce produced.

Roux blanc

ROUX BLANC

Melt the butter slowly, then quickly stir in the flour. Continue cooking over a low heat for 1-2 minutes before removing from the heat and gradually adding hot liquid. This method will produce a white sauce.

Roux blond

ROUX BLOND

Made in the same way but the flour and butter are cooked for 3-4 minutes until they turn a pale straw color.

ROUX BRUN

Again the butter and flour are cooked, but this time for 7-8 minutes until a pale nut brown color. Stir continuously as it will easily burn.

Roux brun

BEURRE MANIÉ

If you have an unknown quantity of liquid to thicken, perhaps the liquid leftover from a casserole or pot roast, then this method is ideal. Equal quantities of flour and butter are blended together, then small pea-sized pieces are stirred into the hot liquid, brought back to the boil and stirred until thickened.

Beurre manié

CORNSTARCH

A fine chalky flour ground from corn, 1 tbsp will thicken ½ pint of liquid. Blend the cornstarch to a paste with 2 tbsp of cold water, then stir into the hot liquid and cook for 1-2 minutes until thickened.

cornstarch

ARROWROOT

A powdery starch derived from the roots of the maranta plant. Used in a similar way to cornstarch it will give a clearer sauce. Remove from the heat as soon as it thickens as it can be unstable.

arrowroot

EGG YOLKS AND CREAM

Blended egg yolks and cream make a rich sauce. Two egg yolks blended with 3-4 tbsp of cream will thicken 1 cup of liquid. Stir a little hot sauce into the egg and cream mixture, then return to the rest of the liquid. Stir over a gentle heat until the sauce coats the back of a spoon. For extra care, cook in a double boiler or in a bowl over a saucepan of hot water.

egg yolks and cream

Preparing Tomatoes

Flame-skinning tomatoes is the simplest and quickest method.

1 Skewer one tomato at a time on a metal fork and hold in a gas flame for 1–2 minutes, turning it until the skin splits and wrinkles.

2 Set aside the tomatoes until cool enough to handle, then slip off and discard the skins.

3 Halve the tomatoes, then scoop out the seeds using a tsp.

4 Finely chop the tomatoes using a small sharp knife and use as desired.

COOK'S TIP

If you don't have a gas stove, simply place the tomatoes in a bowl of boiling water for 30–60 seconds, until the skin splits. Rinse the tomatoes under cold water, then peel.

Preparing Cucumber

Cucumber can be cut into strips and then softened for use in delicate salsas by salting.

1 Trim the ends from the cucumber and cut it into 1-in lengths, then slice each piece lengthwise into thin strips.

2 Place the cucumber slices in a colander and sprinkle with 1 tsp salt. Let sit for 5 minutes, until wilted.

3 Wash the cucumber slices well under cold running water, then drain and pat them dry with paper towels.

Preparing Chilies

The hottest chilies need very careful handling – just follow these simple steps. If you do touch chilies, wash your hands thoroughly.

Peeling Bell Peppers

Peppers are delicious added raw to salads. However, roasting them first softens the flesh and gives them a delicious warm flavor.

1 To remove the skin from habanero chilies, skewer the chilies, one at a time, on a metal fork and hold over a gas flame for 2–3 minutes, turning the chili until the skin blackens and blisters.

2 Let the chilies cool for a few minutes, then use a clean dish towel to rub off the skins.

1 Preheat the broiler. Place the peppers on a baking sheet and broil for 8–12 minutes, turning regularly, until the skins have blackened and blistered.

2 Place the peppers in a bowl and cover with a clean dish towel. Set aside. Leave for 5 minutes so the steam helps to lift the skin away from the flesh.

3 Try not to touch the chilies with your bare hands; use a fork to hold them and slice them open with a sharp knife.

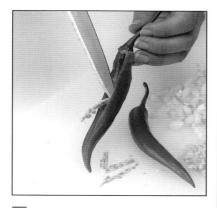

4 Even the less hot varieties of chilies can be fairly fiery. To reduce the heat, cut the chilies in half and scrape out the seeds using the tip of a knife.

3 When the peppers are cool enough to handle, pierce a hole in the bottom of each one and gently squeeze out the juices into a bowl.

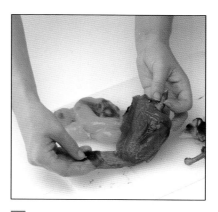

4 Peel off and discard the skins from the peppers and then chop or slice as desired.

Keeping Sauces Warm

There is nothing more unappetizing than a congealed sauce, so keeping sauces warm successfully is essential. It can sometimes be tricky: the more delicate cream- and butter-based sauces curdle easily, while flour-based sauces may thin with prolonged heating. Follow the advice below to prevent a skin forming while keeping the sauce at a reasonable temperature.

COOK'S TIP
All these types of sauces can also be kept warm in a vacuum flask. Make sure the flask is reasonably new and free of any stains or lingering smells. You may find that keeping the sauce in a flask alters its flavor, so this method should only be used as a last resort. Remember to heat the flask first with boiling water before gently pouring in the warm sauce.

1 Pour the sauce into a double boiler or a bowl suspended over a pan of hot, not boiling, water. To prevent a skin forming on a cream and butter sauce, cover the surface of the sauce with buttered wax paper or plastic wrap.

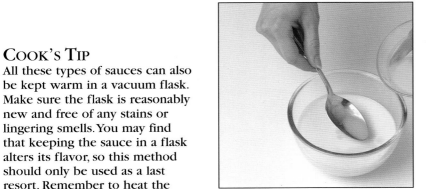

2 For flour-based sauces, spoon over a little melted butter.

3 For sweet sauces, sprinkle the surface with sugar.

Bread Sauce

Smooth and surprisingly delicate, this old-fashioned sauce is traditionally served with roast chicken, turkey and game birds. If you'd prefer a less strong flavor, reduce the number of cloves and add a little freshly grated nutmeg instead.

Serves 6

INGREDIENTS
4 cloves
1 small onion
bay leaf
1¹/₄ cup milk
2 cups fresh white breadcrumbs
1 tbsp butter
1 tbsp light cream
salt and pepper

breadcrumbs

milk

cloves

cream

onion

butter

bay leaf

1 Peel the onion and stick the cloves into it. Put it into a saucepan with the bay leaf and pour in the milk.

2 Bring to a boil then remove from the heat and steep for 15–20 minutes. Remove the bay leaf and onion.

3 Return to the heat and stir in the crumbs. Simmer for 4–5 minutes or until thick and creamy.

4 Stir in the butter and cream, then season to taste.

Horseradish Sauce

This light, creamy sauce has a piquant, peppery flavor that's spiced with just a hint of mustard. It is the classic accompaniment to roast beef, but is perfect, too, with herby sausages and grilled fish.

Serves 6

INGREDIENTS
3 in piece fresh horseradish
1 tbsp lemon juice
2 tsp sugar
$^1/_2$ tsp English mustard powder
$^2/_3$ cup heavy cream

cream

horseradish

mustard

sugar

lemon

1 Scrub and peel the horseradish.

2 Grate the horseradish as finely as you can.

3 Mix together the horseradish, lemon juice, sugar and mustard powder.

4 Whip the cream until it stands in soft peaks then gently fold in the horseradish mixture.

Apple Sauce

Really more of a condiment than a sauce, this tart puree is usually served cold or warm, rather than hot. It's typically served with rice, roast pork or duck, but is also good with cold meats and savory pies.

Serves 6

INGREDIENTS
8 oz tart cooking apples
2 tbsp water
thin strip lemon rind
1 tbsp butter
1–2 tbsp sugar

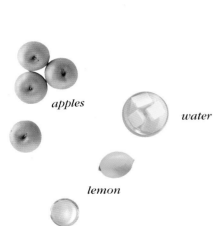

apples

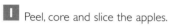

water

lemon

sugar

1 Peel, core and slice the apples.

2 Place the apples in a saucepan with the water and lemon peel. Cook uncovered over a low heat until very soft, stirring occasionally.

3 Remove the lemon rind, then beat to a pulp with a spoon or press through a strainer.

4 Stir in the butter and then add sugar to taste.

Cranberry Sauce

This is the sauce for roast turkey, but don't just keep it for festive occasions. The vibrant color and tart taste are a perfect partner to any white roast meat, and it makes a great addition to a chicken sandwich.

Serves 6

INGREDIENTS
1 orange
8 oz cranberries
1¹/₄ cups sugar

orange

sugar

cranberries

1 Pare the rind thinly from the orange, taking care not to remove any white pith. Squeeze the juice.

2 Place in a saucepan with the cranberries, sugar and ²/₃ cup water.

3 Bring to a boil, stirring until the sugar has dissolved, then simmer for 10–15 minutes or until the berries burst.

4 Remove the rind and allow to cool before serving.

Mint Sauce

Tart, yet sweet, this simple sauce is the perfect foil to rich meat. It's best served, of course, with new season's roast lamb, but is wonderful, too, with grilled lamb chops or pan-fried duck.

Serves 6

INGREDIENTS
small bunch mint
1 tbsp sugar
2 tbsp boiling water
3 tbsp white wine vinegar

white wine vinegar

mint

sugar

1 Strip the leaves from the stalks.

2 Chop the leaves very finely.

3 Place in a bowl with the sugar and pour on the boiling water. Stir well and let stand for 5–10 minutes.

4 Add the vinegar and let stand for 1–2 hours before serving.

Tangy Orange Sauce

SAUCE BIGARADE

A tangy orange sauce for roast duck and rich game. For a full mellow flavor, it is best made with the rich roasting-pan juices, but butter makes an excellent substitute if these aren't available.

Serves 4-6

INGREDIENTS
roasting pan juices or 2 tbsp
   butter
3 tbsp flour
1¼ cups hot stock (preferably
   duck)
½ cup red wine
2 Temple oranges or 2 sweet
   oranges plus 2 tsp lemon juice
1 tbsp orange-flavored liqueur
2 tbsp red currant jelly
salt and pepper

roasting-pan juices

red wine

flour

orange-flavored liqueur

butter

red currant jelly

lemon

oranges

1 Pour off any excess fat from the roasting pan leaving the juices, or melt the butter in a small pan.

2 Sprinkle in the flour and cook, stirring constantly for 4 minutes or until lightly browned.

3 Remove from the heat, blend in the hot stock and wine. Reheat, bring to the boil, stirring constantly. Lower the heat and simmer for 5 minutes.

4 Meanwhile, using a citrus zester, peel the rind thinly from one orange. Squeeze the juice from both oranges.

5 Blanch the rind; place it in a small pan, cover with water and bring to a boil. Cook for 5 minutes, drain and add the rind to the sauce.

6 Add the orange juice, liqueur and jelly to the sauce, stirring until the jelly has dissolved. Season to taste and pour over the carved duckling or game.

Spicy Red Currant Sauce

CUMBERLAND SAUCE

Spicy yet sweet, this red currant sauce is ideal for smoked or cured ham. A string of translucent, jewel-like red currants would make an excellent summery garnish for a dish served with this sauce.

Serves 8

INGREDIENTS
1 lemon
1 orange
2 sugar lumps
1/2 cup port
4 allspice berries
4 cloves
1 tsp mustard seeds
8 oz red currant jelly
2 tsp arrowroot
2 tbsp orange liqueur
pinch of ground ginger

port

red currant jelly   arrowroot

sugar lumps, cloves and allspice berries

lemon

orange liqueur

ground ginger

orange

1 Peel the lemon thinly so that no white pith is removed. Cut into thin strips with a sharp knife or scissors, or peel the lemon with a citrus zester.

2 Blanch the rind: place in a small pan. Cover with water and bring to ta boil. Cook for 5 minutes, drain and reserve the rinds.

3 Wash the orange, then rub it all over with the sugar lumps until they are saturated with oil.

4 In a small pan bring the port, sugar lumps and whole spices to a boil. Remove from the heat and cool. Strain the port into a pan, add the jelly and stir over a low heat until dissolved.

COOK'S TIP
To develop a rich spicy flavor, store this sauce in the fridge for 2-3 days, then bring to room temperature before serving.

5 Blend the arrowroot with the orange liqueur and stir into the sauce. Bring to the boil and cook for 1–2 minutes or until it has thickened.

6 Remove from the heat and add the rinds and ground ginger to taste. Cool to room temperature before serving with hot or cold ham slices or grilled lamb cutlets.

Mushroom and Wine Sauce

SAUCE CHASSEUR

This excellent sauce will transform simple pan-fried or grilled chicken and light meats into a dinner-party dish.

Serves 3–4

INGREDIENTS
2 tbsp butter
1 shallot, finely chopped
4 oz button mushrooms, sliced
1/2 cup white wine
2 tbsp brandy
1 quantity Sauce Espagnole
1 tbsp chopped fresh tarragon or
 chervil

brandy

white wine

butter

shallot

button mushrooms

Sauce Espagnole

chervil

1 Melt the butter and fry the shallot until soft but not brown.

2 Add the mushrooms and sauté until they just begin to brown.

3 Pour in the wine and brandy, and simmer over a medium heat until reduced by half.

4 Add the Espagnole Sauce and herbs and heat through, stirring occasionally. Serve hot with grilled or roast pork, chicken or rabbit.

COOK'S TIP
If you don't mind the gray tinge they give to the color, large mushrooms have more flavor than button ones.

Tartare Sauce

This is an authentic tartare sauce to serve with all kinds of fish, but for a simpler version you could always stir the flavorings into mayonnaise.

Serves 6

INGREDIENTS
2 hard-boiled eggs
1 egg yolk from a large egg
2 tsp lemon juice
3/4 cup olive oil
1 tsp chopped capers
1 tsp chopped gherkin
1 tsp chopped fresh chives
1 tsp chopped fresh parsley
salt and pepper

chives

olive oil

hard-boiled eggs

lemon

gherkin and capers

parsley

egg yolk

1 Halve the hard-boiled eggs, remove the yolks and press them through a strainer into a bowl.

2 Blend in the raw yolk and mix until smooth. Stir in the lemon juice.

3 Add the oil very slowly, a little at a time, whisking constantly. When it begins to thicken, add the oil more quickly to form a thick emulsion.

4 Finely chop one egg white and stir into the sauce with the capers, gherkins and herbs. Season to taste. Serve as an accompaniment to fried or grilled fish.

Hollandaise Sauce

A rich butter sauce for fish and vegetables. The secret of success with this sauce is patience. Work in the butter slowly and thoroughly to give a thick, glossy texture.

Serves 2-3

INGREDIENTS
2 tbsp white wine or tarragon
   vinegar
1 tbsp water
6 black peppercorns
1 bay leaf
1/2 cup butter
2 egg yolks
salt and pepper

bay leaf

egg yolks

*black
peppercorns*

butter

white wine vinegar

1 Place the vinegar, water, peppercorns, and bay leaf in a saucepan. Simmer gently until the liquid has reduced by half. Strain and cool.

2 Cream the butter until soft.

3 In a double saucepan or a bowl sitting over a saucepan of gently simmering, but not boiling, water, beat together the egg yolks and vinegar until light and fluffy.

4 Gradually add the butter, a tiny piece at a time – about the size of a hazelnut will be enough. Whisk quickly until all the butter has been absorbed before adding any more.

5 Season lightly and, if the sauce is too sharp, add a little more butter.

6 For a thinner sauce, stir in 1–2 tablespoons of light cream. Serve immediately with either steamed fish or fresh vegetables.

Rich Brown Sauce

SAUCE ESPAGNOLE

Espagnole is ideal for serving with red meat and game. It also makes a delicious full-flavored base for other sauces, so make double quantity and keep some in the fridge.

Serves 4-6

INGREDIENTS
2 tbsp butter
2 oz bacon pieces or streaky bacon, chopped
2 shallots, chopped
1 carrot, chopped
1 celery stalk, chopped
mushroom trimmings (if available)
2 tbsp flour
2¹/₂ cups hot Brown Stock
1 bouquet garni
2 tbsp tomato paste
1 tbsp sherry (optional)
salt and pepper

1 Melt the butter in a heavy saucepan and fry the bacon for 2–3 minutes. Add the vegetables and cook for another 5–6 minutes until golden.

2 Stir in the flour and cook over a medium heat for 5–10 minutes until it has become a rich brown color.

3 Remove from the heat and gradually blend in the stock.

brown stock

carrot

celery

mushroom trimmings

shallots

sherry

flour

butter

bouquet garni

tomato paste

bacon

4 Slowly bring to the boil, stirring constantly, until the sauce thickens. Add the bouquet garni, tomato paste and seasoning. Reduce the heat and simmer gently for one hour, stirring occasionally.

5 Strain the sauce, pressing the vegetables to extract the juice.

6 Skim off any fat with a metal spoon. Stir in the sherry and adjust the seasoning to taste. Serve with grilled lamb chops, or other red meat.

Creamy Madeira Sauce

NEWBURG SAUCE

This creamy Madeira-flavored sauce will not mask delicate foods and is therefore ideal for shellfish. It also goes well with pan-fried chicken.

Serves 4

INGREDIENTS
1 tbsp butter
1 small shallot, finely chopped
cayenne pepper
1¼ cups heavy cream
4 tbsp Madeira
salt and pepper
3 egg yolks

heavy cream

shallot   *egg yolks*

butter

cayenne pepper   *Madeira*

1 Melt the butter in a double boiler or a bowl placed over a saucepan of simmering water. Cook the shallots until they are soft.

2 Add the cayenne and all but 4 tbsp of the cream. Leave over the simmering water for 10 minutes to reduce slightly.

3 Stir in the Madeira.

4 Beat the yolks with the remaining cream and stir into the hot sauce. Continue stirring over barely simmering water until thickened. Season to taste. Spoon over seafood or chicken, reserving some for pouring, and serve immediately. Garnish with fresh herbs.

COOK'S TIP

For a luxurious festive look, stir in 1–2 tbsp pink or black lumpfish roe.

White Sauce

This basic recipe is wonderfully adaptable, but can be bland, so always taste and season carefully.

Serves 6

INGREDIENTS
2¹/₂ cups milk
2 tbsp flour
2 tbsp butter
salt and pepper

flour

milk

butter

salt and pepper

1 Warm the milk in a saucepan over a low heat, but do not boil.

2 In a separate saucepan melt the butter, then stir in the flour and cook gently for 1–2 minutes. Do not allow the roux to brown.

3 Remove from the heat and gradually blend in the milk, stirring vigorously after each addition to prevent lumps forming. Reheat, bring to a boil slowly and constantly stir until the sauce thickens. Simmer gently for another 3–4 minutes to thicken. Season to taste

VARIATIONS
PARSLEY SAUCE is traditionally served with bacon, fish and fava beans. Stir in 2 tbsp finely chopped fresh parsley.

CHEESE SAUCE may be used for egg and vegetable gratins. Stir in ¹/₂ cup finely grated sharp Cheddar and ¹/₂ tsp prepared mustard.

COOK'S TIP
For a thicker sauce that will coat a spoon, increase the amount of flour to ¹/₂ cup and the butter to 4 tbsp.

Béchamel Sauce

The creamy mellowness of the béchamel makes it ideal for lasagne as well as a base for many fish, egg and vegetable dishes.

Serves 4

INGREDIENTS
1 small onion
1 small carrot
1 celery stalk
1 bouquet garni
6 black peppercorns
pinch freshly grated nutmeg or
  blade of mace
1¼ cups milk
2 tbsp butter
2 tbsp flour
2 tbsp light cream
salt and pepper

bouquet garni

butter

black peppercorns
and nutmeg

cream

onion

milk

flour

carrot

celery

1 Peel and finely chop the vegetables.

2 Put the milk, vegetables and flavorings in a saucepan. Bring to a boil. Remove from the heat, cover and allow to steep for 30 minutes.

3 Melt the butter in a saucepan, remove from the heat and stir in the flour. Return to the heat and cook for 1–2 minutes.

4 Reheat the flavored milk to almost boiling. Strain into a heat-proof pitcher, pressing the vegetables with the back of a spoon to extract the juices.

5 Rebove from the heat, gradually blend the milk into the roux, stirring vigorously after each addition.

6 Reheat, bring to a boil and stir constantly until the sauce thickens. Simmer gently for 3–4 minutes. Remove from the heat, adjust the seasoning to taste and stir in the cream.

Herb Butter Sauce

SAUCE BEARNAISE

For dedicated meat-eaters, this sauce adds a note of sophistication without swamping your grilled or pan-fried steak.

Serves 2-3

INGREDIENTS
3 tbsp white wine vinegar
2 tbsp water
1 small onion, finely chopped
a few fresh tarragon and chervil
    sprigs
1 bay leaf
6 crushed black peppercorns
1/2 cup butter
2 egg yolks
1 tbsp chopped fresh herbs, e.g.
    tarragon, parsley, chervil
salt and pepper

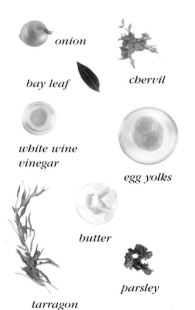

onion

bay leaf *chervil*

*white wine
vinegar*

egg yolks

butter

parsley

tarragon

1 Place the vinegar, water, onion, herbs and peppercorns in a saucepan. Simmer gently until the liquid is reduced by half. Strain and cool.

2 Cream the butter until soft.

3 In a double saucepan or a bowl over a saucepan of gently simmering water, whisk the egg yolks and liquid until light and fluffy.

4 Gradually add the butter, half a teaspoonful at a time. Whisk until all the butter has been incorporated before adding any more.

5 Add the chopped herbs and season to taste.

6 Serve warm, not hot, beside a grilled steak or allow a good spoonful to melt over new potatoes.

Savory Pouring Sauce

SAUCE VELOUTÉ

A smooth, velvety sauce based on a white stock made from fish, vegetable or meat. Choose whichever is suitable for the dish you are serving.

Serves 4

INGREDIENTS
2¹/₂ cups white stock
2 tbsp butter
2 tbsp flour
2 tbsp light cream
salt and pepper

butter

white stock

salt and pepper

light cream

flour

1 Warm the stock but do not boil. In another pan melt the butter and stir in the flour. Cook over a moderate heat for 3–4 minutes until a pale, straw color, stirring constantly.

2 Remove the pan from the heat and gradually blend in the stock. Return to the heat and bring to the boil, stirring constantly, until the sauce thickens.

3 Continue to cook at a very low simmer, stirring occasionally, until reduced by about a quarter.

4 Skim the surface during cooking or pour through a very fine strainer.

5 Just before serving, remove from the heat and stir in the cream. Season to taste.

Green Peppercorn Sauce

Green peppercorns in brine are a better choice than the dry-packed type because they give a more rounded flavor.

Serves 3-4

INGREDIENTS
1 tbsp green peppercorns in
   brine, drained
1 small onion, finely chopped
2 tbsp butter
1¼ cups light stock
juice of ½ lemon
1 tbsp beurre manié
3 tbsp heavy cream
1 tsp Dijon mustard
salt and pepper

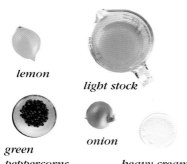

lemon

light stock

*green
peppercorns*

onion

heavy cream

Dijon mustard

beurre manié

butter

1 Dry the peppercorns on paper towels, then crush lightly under the blade of a heavy-bladed knife.

2 Soften the onion in the butter, add the stock and lemon juice and simmer for 15 minutes.

3 Whisk in the beurre manié a little at a time, and continue to cook until the sauce thickens.

4 Reduce the heat and stir in the peppercorns, cream and mustard. Season to taste. Serve hot with pork-rib chops and buttered pasta.

Barbecue Sauce

Brush this sauce liberally over chicken drumsticks, chops or kebabs before cooking on the barbecue, or serve as a hot or cold accompaniment to hot dogs and burgers.

Serves 4

INGREDIENTS
2 tbsp vegetable oil
1 large onion, chopped
2 garlic cloves, crushed
14 oz can tomatoes
2 tbsp Worcestershire sauce
1 tbsp white wine vinegar
3 tbsp honey
1 tsp mustard powder
$1/2$ tsp chili seasoning or mild chili powder
salt and pepper

honey

white wine vinegar

onion

vegetable oil

tomatoes

Worcestershire sauce

garlic

mustard powder

mild chili powder

1 Heat the oil and fry the onions and garlic until soft.

2 Stir in the remaining ingredients and simmer, uncovered, for 15–20 minutes, stirring occasionally. Cool slightly.

3 Pour into a food processor or blender and process until smooth.

4 Press through a strainer if you prefer and adjust the seasoning.

Cider and Apple Cream

This sauce works excellently with grilled pork accompanied by its own garnish of rosy, glazed apple rings.

Serves 4

INGREDIENTS
3 tbsp butter
2 shallots, chopped
1 celery stalk, chopped
1 carrot, chopped
2 tbsp flour
$1^7/_8$ cup hot, white stock
$1^1/_4$ cups dry cider
4 tbsp Calvados
4 tbsp light cream
salt and pepper

FOR THE GLAZED APPLE RINGS
2 tbsp butter
1 eating apple, cored and sliced
1 tbsp sugar

flour

carrot

butter

white stock

shallots

sugar

celery

Calvados

eating apple

dry cider

light cream

1 Melt the butter in a pan, add the shallots, celery and carrot. Sauté over a gentle heat until soft but not colored.

2 Sprinkle over the flour and cook over a low heat for 1–2 minutes, constantly making sure you stir.

3 Remove the sauce from the heat and gradually blend in the stock, cider and Calvados.

4 Return to the heat and bring to a boil, stirring constantly until the sauce thickens. Then simmer, uncovered, until it is reduced by half.

5 Strain into a clean pan and add the cream. Heat through and taste before seasoning as it can be salty.

VARIATION
You could also use cider and apple cream sauce as an alternative to gravy with a traditional pork roast.

6 For the glazed apples, melt the butter in a frying pan. Add the apple slices in a single layer and sprinkle with sugar. Cook over a moderate heat, turning occasionally, until soft and lightly caramelized. Serve the sauce with pan fried or grilled pork and veal, and garnish with the glazed apples.

Lemon and Tarragon Sauce

The sharpness of lemon and mild anise flavor of tarragon add zest to chicken, egg and steamed vegetable dishes.

Serves 4

INGREDIENTS
1 lemon
small bunch fresh tarragon
1 shallot, finely chopped
6 tbsp white wine
1 quantity Velouté Sauce (see page 38)
3 tbsp heavy cream
2 tbsp brandy
salt and pepper

shallot

Velouté Sauce

tarragon

lemon

white wine

brandy

1 Thinly pare the rind from the lemon, taking care not to remove any white pith. Squeeze the juice into a pan.

2 Discard the coarse stalks from the tarragon. Chop the leaves and add all but 15 ml/1 tbsp to the pan with the lemon rind, shallot and wine.

3 Simmer gently until the liquid is reduced by half. Strain into a clean pan.

4 Add the Velouté Sauce, cream, brandy and reserved tarragon. Heat through, taste and adjust the seasoning if necessary.

COOK'S TIPS
Wrap pieces of boned chicken breast with bacon slices and secure with toothpicks, before pan frying.

Chinese-style Sweet and Sour Sauce

A great family favorite that adds a taste of the Orient.

Serves 4

INGREDIENTS
1 carrot
1 green bell pepper
1 tbsp vegetable oil
1 small onion, chopped
1 garlic clove, crushed
$1/2$ in piece fresh ginger, peeled and grated
$1/2$ tbsp cornstarch
$1^1/_4$ cups white stock
2 tbsp tomato paste
1 tbsp dark brown sugar
2 tbsp white wine vinegar
2 tbsp rice wine or sherry
salt and pepper
stir-fried pork or chicken, to serve
rice or noodles, to serve
cucumber, to garnish

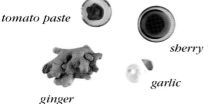

green bell pepper

white

white wine vinegar

onion

carrot

cornstarch

dark brown sugar

tomato paste

sherry

ginger

garlic

1 Peel the carrot and cut into matchstick-sized strips. Quarter the pepper, discard the stalks, seeds and membrane and cut into strips.

2 Heat the oil and fry the onion and garlic until soft but not brown. Add the carrot, pepper and ginger and cook for another minute. Remove from the heat.

3 Blend the cornfstarch with a little stock and add to the vegetables, together with the remaining ingredients.

4 Stir over a moderate heat until the mixture boils and thickens. Simmer uncovered for 2–3 minutes until the vegetables are just tender. Adjust the seasoning and serve with strips of stir-fried pork or chicken and with rice or noodles. Garnish with cucmber.

Satay Dip

A deliciously pungent sauce. It tastes great served with satay sticks and is equally good as a dip for crisp vegetables.

Serves 6

INGREDIENTS
1 cup roasted, unsalted peanuts
3 tbsp vegetable oil
1 small onion, coarsely chopped
2 garlic cloves, crushed
1 red chili, seeded and chopped
1 in piece fresh ginger, peeled
  and chopped
2 in piece lemon grass, coarsely
  chopped
$^1/_2$ tsp ground cumin
3 tbsp chopped fresh cilantro
  stalks
1 tbsp sesame oil
$^3/_4$ cup coconut milk
2 tbsp thick soy sauce
  (kecap manis)
2 tsp lime juice
salt and pepper
lime wedges and chives, to garnish

garlic

red chili

limes

coconut milk

ginger

vegetable oil

onion

ground cumin

thick soy sauce

lemon grass

cilantro

sesame oil

unsalted peanuts

1 Rub the husks from the peanuts in a clean tea towel.

2 Grind to a smooth paste with 2 tbsp vegetable oil in a blender or food processor. Set to one side.

3 Place the next seven ingredients in the blender or food processor and process to a fairly smooth paste.

4 Heat the remaining vegetable oil with the sesame oil in a small saucepan and add the onion paste. Cook over a low heat for about 10–15 minutes, stirring occasionally.

5 Stir in the peanut paste, coconut milk, soy sauce and lime juice, and keep stirring while it heats through.

6 Adjust the seasoning, then pour into small bowls or saucers. Serve warm with broiled, skewered chicken or pork, or with small spicy meatballs, garnished with lime wedges and chives.

Creamy Dill and Mustard Sauce

This sauce will give a tangy, Scandinavian flavor to grilled fish dishes.

Serves 3-4

INGREDIENTS
2 tbsp butter
1½ tbsp flour
1¼ cups hot fish stock
1 tbsp white wine vinegar
3 tbsp chopped fresh dill
1 tbsp whole grain mustard
2 tsp sugar
2 egg yolks
salt and pepper

flour

sugar

dill

fish stock

white wine vinegar

whole grain mustard

egg yolks

butter

1 Melt the butter and stir in the flour. Cook for 1–2 minutes over a low heat, stirring constantly.

2 Remove from the heat and gradually blend in the hot stock. Return to the heat, bring to a boil, stirring constantly, then simmer for 2–3 minutes.

3 Remove from the heat and beat in the vinegar, dill, mustard and sugar.

4 Using a fork, beat the yolks in a small bowl and gradually add a small quantity of hot sauce. Return to the pan, whisking vigorously. Continue whisking over a very low heat for another minute. Serve with grilled fillets of sole, sand-dab or halibut.

Orange and Caper Sauce

A wonderfully sweet-sour sauce to add zest to otherwise plain white fish.

Serves 3-4

INGREDIENTS
2 tbsp butter
1 onion, chopped
fish bones and trimmings
1 tsp black peppercorns
1¼ cups dry white wine
2 small oranges
1 tbsp capers, drained
4 tbsp crème fraîche
salt and pepper

fish bones and trimmings

onion

crème fraîche   *dry white wine*

butter   *black peppercorns*

oranges   *capers*

1 Melt the butter and add the onion. Sauté over a moderate heat until the onion is lightly browned.

2 Add the fish trimmings and peppercorns, and pour in the wine. Cover and simmer gently for 30 minutes.

3 Using a serrated knife, peel the oranges, making sure all the white pith is removed. Ease the segments away from the membrane.

4 Strain the stock into a clean saucepan. Add the capers and orange segments together with any juice and heat through. Lower the heat and gently stir in the crème fraîche and seasoning. Serve hot with grilled or poached skate wings or fillets of sole.

Watercress Cream

The delicate green color of this cream sauce looks wonderful against pink-fleshed fish like salmon or salmon trout.

Serves 4

INGREDIENTS
2 bunches watercress
2 tbsp butter
2 shallots, chopped
2 tbsp flour
²/₃ cup hot fish stock
²/₃ cup dry white wine
1 tsp anchovy extract
²/₃ cup single cream
salt
pinch cayenne pepper
lemon juice

anchovy extract

watercress

flour

shallots

cayenne pepper

light cream

dry white wine

fish stock

butter

1 Trim the watercress of any bruised leaves and coarse stalks. Blanch in boiling water for 5 minutes.

2 Drain and refresh the watercress under cold running water. In a strainer, press well with the back of a kitchen spoon to remove excess moisture, then chop finely.

3 Melt the butter and sauté the shallots until soft. Stir in the flour and cook for 1–2 minutes.

4 Turn off the heat and gradually blend in the stock, followed by the wine. Return to the heat, bring to the boil, stirring constantly, and simmer gently for 2–3 minutes.

VARIATION
To make arugula cream sauce, replace the watercress with 1 oz arugula leaves.

5 Strain into a clean pan, then add the watercress, anchovy extract and cream. Warm through over a low heat.

6 Season with salt and cayenne pepper and lemon juice to taste. Serve immediately with broiled, barbecued or poached salmon.

Garlic and Chili Dip

Plainly cooked fish can sometimes be rather bland. This sauce will spice it up. Or try it with lightly battered, deep-fried vegetables.

Serves 4

INGREDIENTS
1 small red chili
1 in piece fresh ginger
2 garlic cloves
1 tsp mustard powder
1 tbsp chili sauce
2 tbsp olive oil
2 tbsp light soy sauce
juice of two limes
2 tbsp chopped fresh parsley
salt and pepper

mustard powder *parsley* *red chili* *ginger* *light soy sauce* *chili sauce* *limes* *garlic*

1 Halve the chili, remove the seeds, stalk and membrane, and chop finely. Peel and coarsely chop the ginger.

2 Crush the chili, ginger, garlic and mustard powder to a paste, using a pestle and mortar.

3 In a bowl, mix together all the remaining ingredients, except the parsley Add the paste and blend it in. Cover and chill for 24 hours.

4 Stir in the parsley and season to taste. It is best to serve in small individual bowls for dipping.

COOK'S TIP

Large shrimps are ideal served with this sauce. Remove the shell but leave the tails intact so there is something to hold on to for dipping.

Saffron Cream

The subtle flavor and coloring of this sauce marries well with steamed or pan-fried scallops in a freshly-baked party shell.

Serves 4

INGREDIENTS
pinch saffron threads
2 tbsp hot water
2 tbsp butter
2 shallots, finely chopped
6 tbsp dry white wine
4 tbsp heavy cream
1 quantity hot fish Velouté Sauce
    (see page 38)
2 egg yolks
salt and pepper
fresh chervil, to garnish

heavy cream *egg yolks*

Velouté Sauce *butter*

shallots

saffron threads

dry white wine

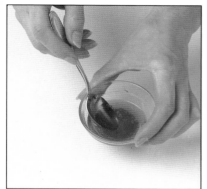

1 Soak the saffron threads in the water for 15 minutes.

2 Melt the butter and sauté the shallot until softened, add the wine and simmer gently until reduced by half.

3 Strain in the saffron water, add the cream, and cook very gently for about 2 minutes.

4 Blend the egg yolks with a little hot Velouté Sauce, remove from the heat and whisk, with the remaining sauce, into the wine and cream. Season lightly.

Maître d'Hôtel Butter

Some fish have such delicate flavor it's a pity to mask them with heavy sauces. This subtle butter, and the variations below, make alternative accompaniments.

Serves 4-6

INGREDIENTS
1/2 cup softened butter
2 tbsp parsley, finely chopped
1/2 tsp lemon juice
cayenne pepper
salt and pepper

parsley

lemon

cayenne pepper

butter

1 Beat the butter until creamy, then beat in the parsley, lemon juice and cayenne pepper, and season lightly.

2 Spread the butter 1/4 in thick on to aluminium foil, chill then cut into shapes with a knife or fancy cutter.

VARIATIONS

Lemon and Lime Butter
Add 1 tbsp finely grated lemon or lime rind and 1 tbsp juice to the butter.

Herb Butter
Replace the parsley with 2 tbsp chopped, mint, chives or tarragon.

Garlic Butter
Add 2 skinned and crushed cloves of garlic to the softened butter with 1–2 tbsp chopped parsley.

Anchovy Butter
Add 6 anchovy fillets, drained of oil and mashed with a fork, to the softened butter. Season with pepper only.

Mustard Butter
Add 2 tsp English mustard powder and 2 tbsp chopped chives to the butter.

3 Alternatively, form into a roll, wrap in plastic wrap or aluminium foil and chill, then cut off slices as required.

COOK'S TIP
These butters will keep in the fridge for several days, and will also freeze, but make sure you wrap them well to avoid any loss of flavor.

Pesto Sauce

There is nothing more evocative of the warmth of Italy than a good homemade pesto. Serve generous spoonfuls with your favorite pasta.

Serves 3-4

INGREDIENTS
2 cups tightly packed basil leaves
2 garlic cloves, crushed
2 tbsp pine nuts
1/2 cup olive oil
2/3 cup Parmesan cheese, finely grated
salt and pepper

garlic

Parmesan cheese

pine nuts

olive oil

basil

1 Using a mortar and pestle, grind the basil, garlic, pine nuts and seasoning to a fine paste.

2 Transfer the mixture to a bowl and whisk in the oil a little at a time.

3 Add the cheese and blend well. Adjust the seasoning to taste.

4 Alternatively, place the basil, garlic, pine nuts and seasoning in a food processor and grind as finely as possible.

5 With the food processor on, slowly add the oil in a thin stream to make a smooth paste.

6 Add the cheese and pulse quickly 3–4 times. Adjust the seasoning if necessary and heat gently.

VARIATION
Pesto also makes an excellent dressing on small new potatoes. Serve while still hot or allow to cool to room temperature.

Rich Tomato Sauce

For a full tomato flavor and rich red color use only really ripe tomatoes. Fresh plum tomatoes are an excellent choice if you can find them.

Serves 4-6

INGREDIENTS
2 tbsp olive oil
1 large onion, chopped
2 garlic cloves, crushed
1 carrot, finely chopped
1 celery stalk, finely chopped
1½ lb tomatoes, peeled and
  chopped
⅔ cup red wine
⅔ cup vegetable stock
1 bouquet garni
1 tbsp tomato paste
½–1 tsp sugar
salt and pepper

vegetable stock

onion

carrot

red wine

olive oil

garlic

tomato paste

tomatoes

celery

bouquet garni

1 Heat the oil and sauté the onion and garlic until soft. Add the carrot and celery and continue to cook, stirring occasionally, until golden.

2 Stir in the tomatoes, wine, stock, bouquet garni and seasoning. Bring to a boil, cover and simmer for 45 minutes, stirring occasionally.

3 Remove the bouquet garni and adjust the seasoning, adding sugar and tomato paste as necessary.

4 Serve the sauce as it is or, for a smoother texture, purée in a blender or food processor, or press through a strainer. Spoon over sliced zucchini or whole fava beans.

Gorgonzola & Walnut Sauce

This is a very quick and very luscious, creamy sauce. Serve with pasta and a green salad for a delicious lunch or supper.

Serves 2

INGREDIENTS

4 tbsp butter
2 oz button mushrooms, sliced
5 oz Gorgonzola cheese
$^2/_3$ cup sour cream
salt and pepper
1 oz Pecorino cheese, grated
$^1/_2$ cup broken walnut pieces

sour cream

walnuts

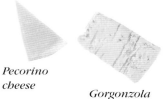

button mushrooms

Pecorino cheese

Gorgonzola cheese

1 Melt the butter and gently fry the mushrooms until lightly browned.

2 With a fork, mash together the Gorgonzola, cream and seasoning.

3 Stir in the mushroom mixture and heat gently until melted.

4 Finally stir in the Pecorino cheese and the walnut pieces.

COOK'S TIP

For an impressive vegetable dish, layer with lightly cooked, thickly sliced potatoes. Sprinkle with more Pecorino cheese and bake at 350°F for 1 hour.

Sweet Pepper & Chili Sauce

A mellow, warming sauce, ideal with pasta. For a more extravagant supper dish add thickly sliced chorizo sausage with the sun-dried tomatoes.

Serves 3–4

INGREDIENTS
2 tbsp olive oil
1 onion, chopped
1 garlic clove, crushed
2 large red or orange bell
    peppers, seeded and finely
    chopped
1 tsp chili seasoning
1 tbsp paprika
$^{1}/_{2}$ tsp dried thyme
1 8 oz can chopped tomatoes
$1^{1}/_{4}$ cups vegetable stock
$^{1}/_{2}$ tsp sugar
salt and pepper
2 tbsp sun-dried tomatoes in oil,
    drained and chopped

onion

olive oil

garlic

red pepper

paprika

thyme

chopped tomatoes

sun-dried tomatoes

1 Heat the oil and sauté the onion, garlic and peppers for 4–5 minutes or until lightly browned.

2 Add the chili, paprika and thyme and cook for another minute.

3 Stir in the tomatoes, stock, sugar and seasoning, and bring to a boil. Cover and simmer for 30 minutes or until soft, adding more stock if necessary.

4 Ten minutes before the end of cooking, add the sun-dried tomatoes. Serve hot with freshly cooked pasta.

Spicy Tuna Dip

A piquant sauce – use more oil for a sauce or dip, less as a filling for hard-boiled eggs, tomatoes or celery stalks.

Serves 6

INGREDIENTS
1 3 oz can tuna in oil
olive oil
4 hard-boiled eggs
3 oz pitted green olives
2 oz can anchovy fillets, drained
3 tbsp capers, drained
2 tsp Dijon mustard
pepper
parsley, to garnish

tuna

anchovy fillets

eggs

green olives

olive oil

Dijon mustard

1 Drain the tuna and add olive oil to the drained oil to make 6 tbsp in all.

2 Halve the hard-boiled eggs, remove the yolks and then place in a blender or food processor.

3 Reserve a few olives for garnishing, then add the rest to the blender together with the remaining ingredients. Blend until smooth. Season with pepper to taste.

4 Spoon into a bowl and garnish with the reserved olives and parsley. Serve with bread sticks for dipping.

Mousseline Sauce

A truly luscious sauce, subtly flavored, rich and creamy.

Serves 4

INGREDIENTS
1 quantity Hollandaise sauce (see page 28) *or* for a less rich sauce:
  2 egg yolks
  1 tbsp lemon juice
  6 tbsp softened butter
6 tbsp heavy cream
salt and pepper

lemon

heavy cream

butter

egg yolks

1 If you are not using prepared Hollandaise, make the sauce: whisk the yolks and lemon juice in a bowl over a pan of barely simmering water until very thick and fluffy.

2 Whisk in the butter, but only a very little at a time, until it is thoroughly absorbed and the sauce has the consistency of mayonnaise.

3 Whisk the cream until stiff.

4 Fold into the warm Hollandaise or prepared sauce and adjust the seasoning. You can add a little more lemon juice for extra tang. Serve as a dip with prepared artichokes or artichoke hearts.

Walnut Sauce with Tagliatelle

An unusual sauce that would make this a spectacular dinner party starter.

Serves 4–6

INGREDIENTS

2 thick slices whole-wheat bread
1¼ cups milk
2½ cups walnut pieces
1 garlic clove, crushed
½ cup freshly grated Parmesan cheese
6 tbsp olive oil, plus extra for tossing the pasta
salt and pepper
⅓ cup heavy cream (optional)
1 lb tagliatelle
2 tbsp chopped fresh parsley

tagliatelle

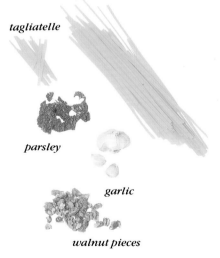

parsley

garlic

walnut pieces

VARIATION

Add ¾ cup pitted black olives to the food processor with the other ingredients for a richer, more piquant sauce. The Greek-style olives have the most flavor.

1 Cut the crusts off the bread and soak in the milk until the milk is all absorbed.

2 Preheat the oven to 375°F. Spread the walnuts on a baking sheet and toast in the oven for 5 minutes. Leave to cool.

3 Place the bread, walnuts, garlic, Parmesan cheese, and olive oil in a food processor and blend until smooth. Season to taste with salt and pepper. Stir in the cream, if using.

4 Cook the pasta in plenty of boiling salted water, drain, and toss with a little olive oil. Divide the pasta equally between 4 bowls and place a dollop of sauce on each portion. Sprinkle liberally with parsley.

Tomato and Clam Sauce with Spaghetti

Small sweet clams make this a delicately succulent sauce. Mussels would make a good substitute, but don't be tempted to use seafood pickled in vinegar – the result will be inedible!

Serves 4

INGREDIENTS
2 lb live small clams, or 2 × 14 oz
    cans clams in brine, drained
6 tbsp olive oil
2 garlic cloves, crushed
1 lb 5 oz canned chopped tomatoes
3 tbsp chopped fresh parsley
salt and pepper
1 lb spaghetti

spaghetti

olive oil

parsley

garlic

clams

1 If using live clams, place them in a bowl of cold water and rinse several times to remove any grit or sand. Drain.

2 Heat the oil in a saucepan and add the clams. Stir over a high heat until the clams open. Throw away any that do not open. Transfer the clams to a bowl with a perforated spoon.

3 Reduce the clam juice left in the pan to almost nothing by boiling fast; this will also concentrate the flavor. Add the garlic and fry until golden. Pour in the tomatoes, bring to a boil, and cook for 3–4 minutes until reduced. Stir in the clam mixture or canned clams, and half the parsley and heat through. Season.

4 Cook the pasta in plenty of boiling salted water according to the manufacturer's instructions. Drain well and transfer to a warm serving dish. Pour over the sauce and sprinkle with the remaining parsley.

Creamy Gruyère Sauce

Gruyère gives this sauce a sweet nutty flavor and it melts wonderfully to a rich velvety smoothness.

Serves 6

INGREDIENTS
3 tbsp butter
3 tbsp flour
1⅞ cup hot vegetable or white
   stock
2 egg yolks
1 tsp Dijon mustard
pinch of ground mace
2 tbsp dry sherry
3 oz Gruyère cheese, grated

vegetable stock

dry sherry

ground mace

butter

Gruyère cheese

egg yolks

flour

Dijon mustard

1 Melt the butter and stir in the flour, and cook over a moderate heat for about 1–2 minutes.

2 Remove from the heat and gradually blend in the hot stock. Return to the heat and bring to a boil, stirring constantly until the sauce thickens. Simmer gently for 3–4 minutes.

3 In a small bowl, blend the egg yolks with a little hot sauce.

4 Return to the pan and cook over very low heat for 1–2 minutes. Do not allow to boil. Finally stir in the flavorings and cheese. Season to taste. Serve with steamed broccoli, cauliflower or leeks.

COOK'S TIP
Crisply fried buttered crumbs and flaked or slivered almonds may be sprinkled over for added crunch.

MARINADES

How to Marinate

Marinades are used to add flavor, moisten or tenderize foods, particularly meat. Marinades can be either savory or sweet and are as varied as you want to make them; spicy, fruity, fragrant or exotic. Certain classic combinations always work well with certain foods. Usually, it's best to choose oily marinades for dry foods, such as lean meat or white fish, and wine- or vinegar-based marinades for rich foods with a higher fat content. Most marinades don't contain salt, which can draw out the juices from meat; it's best to add salt just before cooking.

1 Place the food for marinating in a wide dish or bowl, preferably large enough to allow it to lie in a single layer.

2 Mix together the ingredients for the marinade thoroughly.

3 Pour the marinade over the food and turn the food, to coat it evenly.

4 Cover the dish and refrigerate from 30 minutes up to several hours, depending on the recipe, turning the food over occasionally, and spooning the marinade over it.

5 Remove the food with a slotted spoon, or lift it out with tongs, and drain off and reserve the marinade. If necessary, allow the food to come to room temperature before cooking.

6 Use the marinade for basting or brushing the food, during cooking.

Marinades For Barbecues

BASIC BARBECUE MARINADE
This can be used for meat or fish.

1 garlic clove, crushed
3 tbsp sunflower or
　olive oil
3 tbsp dry sherry
1 tbsp Worcestershire
　sauce
1 tbsp dark soy sauce
freshly ground black pepper

HERB MARINADE
This is good for fish, meat or poultry.

$\frac{1}{2}$ cup dry white wine
4 tbsp olive oil
1 tbsp lemon juice
2 tbsp finely chopped fresh herbs,
　such as parsley, thyme, chives or
　basil
freshly ground black pepper

COOK'S TIP
The amount of marinade you
will need depends on the
amount of the food but, as a
rough guide, about $\frac{2}{3}$ cup
should be enough for about
$1\frac{1}{4}$ lb of food.

HONEY CITRUS MARINADE
This is good with fish or chicken.

finely grated zest and juice of
　$\frac{1}{2}$ lime, $\frac{1}{2}$ lemon and $\frac{1}{2}$ small
　orange
3 tbsp sunflower or other light
　oil
2 tbsp clear honey
1 tbsp soy sauce
1 tsp Dijon mustard
freshly ground black pepper

YOGURT SPICE MARINADE
For fish, meats or poultry.

$\frac{2}{3}$ cup plain yogurt
1 small onion, finely chopped
1 garlic clove, crushed
1 tsp finely chopped fresh root
　ginger
1 tsp ground coriander
1 tsp ground cumin
$\frac{1}{2}$ tsp ground turmeric

RED WINE MARINADE
Good with red meats and game.

$\frac{2}{3}$ cup dry red wine
1 tbsp olive oil
1 tbsp red-wine vinegar
2 garlic cloves, crushed
2 dried bay leaves, crumbled
freshly ground black pepper

Red Wine and Juniper Marinade

Marinating develops a rich base for casseroles and stews. This marinade is also excellent for pot-roasted beef.

Serves 4-6

INGREDIENTS
1¹/₂ lb boned leg of lamb, trimmed and cut into 1 in cubes

FOR THE MARINADE:
2 carrots, cut into small sticks
8 oz baby onions or shallots
4 oz button mushrooms
4 rosemary sprigs
8 juniper berries, lightly crushed
8 black peppercorns, lightly crushed
1¹/₄ cups red wine
2 tbsp vegetable oil
²/₃ cup beef stock
2 tbsp beurre manié

baby onions   *red wine*

juniper berries and black peppercorns   *button mushrooms*

carrot

rosemary

1 Place the meat in a bowl, add the vegetables, rosemary and spices then pour over the wine. Cover and leave in a cool place for 45 hours, stirring once or twice during this time.

2 Remove the lamb and vegetables with a slotted spoon and set aside. Strain the marinade into a pitcher.

3 Preheat the oven to 325°F. Heat the oil in a flameproof casserole and fry the meat and vegetables in batches until lightly browned. Pour over the reserved marinade and stock. Cover and cook in the oven for 2 hours.

4 Twenty minutes before the end of cooking stir in the beurre manié, cover and return to the oven. Season to taste before serving.

Chinese-style Marinade with Toasted Sesame Seeds

Toasted sesame seeds bring their distinctive smoky aroma to this Oriental marinade.

Serves 4

INGREDIENTS
1 lb top round steak
2 tbsp sesame seeds
1 tbsp sesame oil
2 tbsp vegetable oil
4 oz small mushrooms, quartered
1 large green bell pepper, seeded and diced
4 scallions, chopped diagonally

FOR THE MARINADE:
2 tsp cornstarch
2 tbsp rice wine or sherry
1 tbsp lemon juice
1 tbsp soy sauce
few drops Tabasco sauce
$1/2$ in piece fresh ginger, peeled and grated
1 garlic clove, crushed

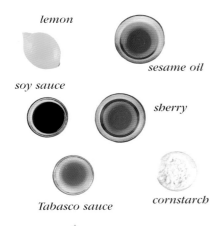

lemon

sesame oil

soy sauce

sherry

Tabasco sauce

cornstarch

garlic *sesame seeds*

ginger

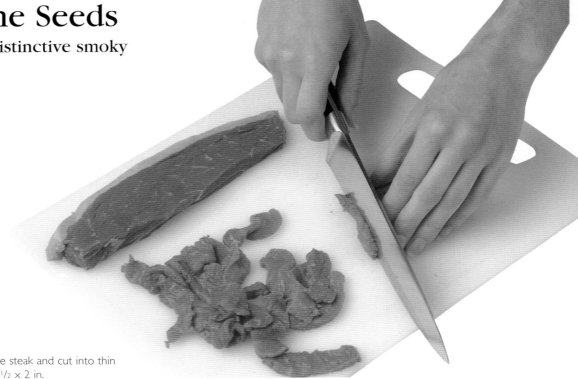

1 Trim the steak and cut into thin strips about $1/2 \times 2$ in.

2 In a bowl, blend the cornstarch with the sherry then stir in the other marinade ingredients. Stir in the beef strips, cover and leave in a cool place for 3-4 hours.

3 Place the sesame seeds in a large frying pan or wok. Cook dry over a moderate heat, shaking the pan until the seeds are golden. Reserve on one side.

4 Heat the oils in the frying pan. Drain the beef, reserving the marinade, and brown a few pieces at a time. Remove with a slotted spoon.

VARIATION
This marinade would also be good with pork or chicken.

5 Add the mushrooms and pepper and sauté for 2–3 minutes, stirring the vegetables constantly. Add the scallions and cook for another minute.

6 Return the beef with the marinade and stir over a moderate heat for another 2 minutes until the ingredients are evenly coated with glaze. Just before serving, sprinkle with sesame seeds.

Summer Herb Marinade

Make the best use of summer herbs in this marinade, which is designed for the barbecue. Any combination may be used depending on what you have on hand, and it can be used with veal, chicken, pork, salmon or lamb.

Serves 4

INGREDIENTS
4 fillets of meat or fish

FOR THE MARINADE:
fresh herb sprigs, e.g. chervil, thyme, parsley, sage, chives, rosemary, oregano
6 tbsp olive oil
3 tbsp tarragon vinegar
1 garlic clove, crushed
2 scallions, chopped
salt and pepper

parsley   *chervil*

garlic

tarragon vinegar   *olive oil*

scallions

chives

thyme

rosemary

oregano

1 Discard any coarse stems or damaged leaves from the herbs, then chop very finely.

2 Mix the herbs with the remaining marinade ingredients.

3 Place the meat or fish in a bowl and pour over the marinade. Cover and leave in a cool place for 4–6 hours.

4 Brush the pieces of meat or fish with the marinade and cook under a hot broiler or over a barbecue grill, turning occasionally, until they are tender. Baste with the marinade while they cook. Serve garnished with fresh herbs.

Ginger and Lime Marinade

This fragrant marinade will guarantee a mouth-watering aroma from the barbecue, and is as delicious with chicken or pork as it is with fish.

Serves 4-6

INGREDIENTS
FOR THE KEBABS:
1¼ lb shrimp and cubed monkfish
selection of prepared vegetables, e.g. red, green or orange bell peppers, zucchini, button mushrooms, red onion, bay leaves, cherry tomtoes

FOR THE MARINADE:
3 limes
1 tbsp green cardamom pods
1 onion, finely chopped
1 in piece fresh ginger, peeled and grated
1 large garlic clove, crushed
3 tbsp olive oil

limes

olive oil

ginger

green cardamoms

onion

garlic

1 Finely grate the rind from one lime and squeeze the juice from all of them.

2 Split the cardamom pods and remove the seeds. Crush with a mortar and pestle or the back of a heavy-bladed knife.

3 Mix all the marinade ingredients together and pour over the meat or fish. Stir in gently, cover and leave in a cool place for 2–3 hours.

4 Thread four skewers alternately with fish and vegetables. Cook slowly under a hot broiler or over a barbecue grill, basting occasionally with the marinade.

Spicy Yogurt Marinade

Plan this dish well in advance; the extra-long marinating time is necessary to develop a really mellow spicy flavor.

Serves 6

INGREDIENTS
6 chicken pieces
juice of 1 lemon
1 tsp salt

FOR THE MARINADE:
1 tsp coriander seeds
2 tsp cumin seeds
6 cloves
2 bay leaves
1 onion, quartered
2 garlic cloves
2 in piece fresh ginger, peeled and
    coarsely chopped
1/2 tsp chili powder
1 tsp turmeric
2/3 cup plainl yogurt
lemon, lime or cilantro, to garnish

lemon

yogurt   *coriander seeds*

ginger

onion

bay leaves

garlic

chili powder

turmeric

cloves   *cumin seeds*

VARIATION
This marinade will also work well brushed over skewers of lamb or pork fillet.

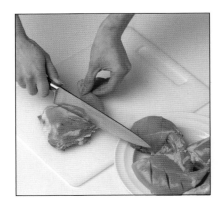

1 Skin the chicken joints and make deep slashes in the fleshiest parts with a sharp knife. Sprinkle over the lemon and salt and rub in.

2 Spread the coriander and cumin seeds, cloves and bay leaves in the bottom of a large frying pan and dry-fry over a moderate heat until the bay leaves are crispy.

3 Cool the spices and grind coarsely with a mortar and pestle.

4 Finely mince the onion, garlic and ginger in a food processor or blender. Add the ground spices, chili, turmeric and yogurt, then strain in the lemon juice from the chicken.

5 Arrange the chicken in a single layer in a roasting tin. Pour over the marinade, then cover and chill for 24–36 hours.

6 Occasionally turn the chicken pieces in the marinade. Preheat the oven to 400°F. Cook the chicken for 45 minutes. Serve hot or cold, garnished with lemon or lime and cilantro leaves.

Winter Spiced Ale Marinade

Serve this on frosty evenings with buttered swede
and crisply cooked cabbage. This marinade can also
be used in a casserole of beef or lamb pieces.

Serves 6

INGREDIENTS
1.4 kg/3 lb top rump beef

FOR THE MARINADE:
1 onion, sliced
2 carrots, sliced
2 celery sticks, sliced
2–3 parsley stalks, lightly crushed
large fresh thyme sprig
2 bay leaves
6 cloves, lightly crushed
1 cinnamon stick
8 black peppercorns
300 ml/^{1}/$_2$ pint/1^1/$_4$ ale
45 ml/3 tbsp vegetable oil
30 ml/2 tbsp beurre manié
salt and pepper

carrot
parsley
vegetable oil
beurre manié
cinnamon
cloves and black peppercorns
thyme
brown ale
onion
bay leaves
celery

1 Place the meat in a polythene bag
placed inside a large deep bowl. Add the
vegetables, herbs and spices, then pour
over the ale. Seal the bag and leave in a
cool place for 5–6 hours.

2 Remove the beef and set aside.
Strain the marinade into a bowl,
reserving the vegetables.

3 Heat the oil in a flame-proof
casserole. Fry the vegetables until lightly
browned, then remove with a slotted
spoon and set aside. Brown the beef all
over in the remaining oil.

4 Preheat the oven to 170°C/ 325°F/
Gas 3. Pour over the reserved marinade
and return the vegetables to the
casserole. Cover the casserole and cook
for 2^1/$_2$ hours. Turn the beef 2 or 3
times in the marinade during this time.

5 To serve, remove the beef and slice
neatly. Arrange on a plate with the
vegetables. Stir the beurre manié into
the marinade and bring to the boil.
Adjust the seasoning before serving.

Rosemary Marinade

If you are serving lamb for your Sunday roast, marinate overnight in the fridge.

Serves 6

INGREDIENTS
3–3½ lb leg of lamb
2 garlic cloves, sliced

FOR THE MARINADE:
1 lemon, sliced
6 rosemary sprigs
4 lemon thyme sprigs
1¼ cups dry white wine
4 tbsp olive oil
salt and pepper
1 tbsp cornstarch

rosemary   *lemon thyme*

lemon

olive oil

dry white wine

garlic

1 Make small cuts over the surface of the lamb and insert a slice of garlic in each, so they sit upright.

2 Place the lamb in a roasting pan, with the lemon slices and herbs sprinkled over it. Mix the remaining marinade ingredients and pour over the lamb. Cover and leave in a cool place for 4–6 hours, turning occasionally. Preheat the oven to 350°F. Roast the lamb for 25 minutes per 1 lb plus 25 minutes more at the end.

3 When the lamb is cooked, transfer to a warmed plate to rest. Drain the excess fat from the pan. Blend the cornstarch with a little cold water and stir into the juices, stir over a moderate heat for 2–3 minutes and season to

VARIATION
You can also use lemon and rosemary marinade for chicken pieces, but you must roast the meat without the marinade because otherwise it will become tough. Use the marinade for making into gravy when the chicken is cooked.

Orange and Green Peppercorn Marinade

This is an excellent light marinade for whole fish. The mouth-watering beauty of a whole fish and the soft-colored marinade needs only a sprig of fresh herb to garnish.

Serves 4

INGREDIENTS
1 3-4 lb whole fish, e.g. salmon
  trout, bass or red snapper,
  cleaned

FOR THE MARINADE:
1 red onion
2 small oranges
6 tbsp light olive oil
2 tbsp cider vinegar
2 tbsp green peppercorns in
  brine, drained
2 tbsp chopped fresh parsley
salt and sugar

oranges

red onion

cider vinegar

parsley

green peppercorns

light olive oil

1 With a sharp knife, slash the fish 3–4 times on both sides.

2 Line an ovenproof dish with foil. Peel and slice the onion and oranges. Lay half in the bottom of the dish, place the fish on top, and cover with the remaining onion and orange.

3 Mix the remaining marinade ingredients and pour over the fish. Cover and stand for 4 hours, occasionally spooning the marinade over the top.

4 Preheat the oven to 350°F. Place the fish in the foil, fold the foil over the fish and seal loosely. Bake for 15 minutes per 450 g/1 lb, plus 15 minutes more.

SALSAS

Tomato and Cilantro Salsa

Salsa is Spanish for sauce, but elsewhere it has come to mean a side dish of finely chopped vegetables or fruits, which really enhances the meals it accompanies.

Serves 6

INGREDIENTS
6 medium tomatoes
1 green chili
2 scallions, chopped
4 in length cucumber, peeled and
   diced
2 tbsp lemon juice
2 tbsp fresh cilantro, chopped
1 tbsp fresh parsley, chopped
salt and pepper

tomatoes
basil
orange pepper
parsley
lemon
scallions
cilantro
garlic
cucumber
capers
green chili

1 Cut a small cross in the stalk end of each tomato. Place in a bowl and cover with boiling water.

2 After 30 seconds or as soon as the skins split, drain and plunge into cold water. Gently slide off the skins. Quarter the tomatoes, remove the seeds and dice the flesh.

3 Halve the chili, remove the stalk, seeds and membrane, and chop finely.

4 Mix together all the ingredients and transfer to a serving bowl. Chill for 1–2 hours before serving.

VARIATIONS

Tomato and Caper Salsa:
Prepare the tomatoes and stir in
the onion and lemon juice. Add
six torn sprigs of basil and 1 tbsp
coarsely chopped capers. Season
to taste.

Tomato and Roast Pepper Salsa:
Prepare 4 tomatoes and stir in the
chili, onion and herbs. Add a
roasted, peeled and diced orange
bell pepper and a crushed garlic
clove. Season to taste.

Green Chili and Coconut Salsa

A sweet-sour salsa that goes well with broiled or barbecued fish.

Serves 6–8

INGREDIENTS
1 small coconut
1 small pineapple
2 green jalapiño chllies
2 in piece lemon grass
4 tbsp natural yogurt
$^1/_2$ tsp salt
2 tbsp chopped cilantror
cilantro sprigs, to garnish

1 Puncture two of the coconut eyes with a screwdriver and drain the milk out from the shell.

2 Crack the shell and prise away the flesh. Peel away the thin brown papery layer and coarsely grate the coconut into a bowl.

3 Cut the rind from the pineapple with a sharp knife and remove the eyes with a potato peeler. Finely chop the flesh and add to the coconut together with any juice.

4 Halve the chilies lengthwise and remove the stalks, seeds and membrane. Chop very finely and stir into the coconut mixture.

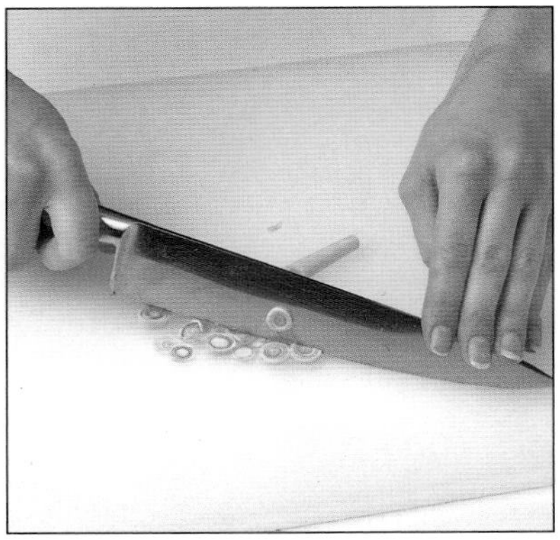

5 Finely chop the lemon grass with a very sharp knife. Add to the coconut mixture and stir in.

6 Add the remaining ingredients and stir well. Spoon into a serving dish and garnish with cilantro sprigs.

Roasted Pepper and Ginger Salsa

Char-broiling to remove the skins will take away any bitterness from the peppers.

Serves 6

INGREDIENTS
1 large red bell pepper
1 large yellow bell pepper
1 large orange bell pepper
1 in piece fresh ginger
1/2 tsp coriander seeds
1 tsp cumin seeds
1 small garlic clove
2 tbsp lime or lemon juice
1 small red onion, finely chopped
2 tbsp chopped fresh cilantro
1 tsp chopped fresh thyme
salt and pepper

red pepper

thyme

yellow pepper

coriander and cumin seeds

orange pepper

garlic

lime

ginger

cilantro

VARIATION
For a spicier version of this recipe, add a green chili, finely chopped, to the pestle and mortar when grinding the ginger and garlic. Or simply add a sprinkle of cayenne pepper to the finished dish before chilling.

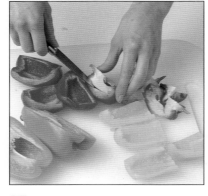

1 Quarter the peppers and remove the stalk, seeds and membranes.

2 Grill the quarters, skin side up, until charred and blistered. Rub away the skins and slice very finely.

3 Peel or scrape the ginger and chop coarsely.

4 Over a moderate heat, gently dry-fry the spices for 30 seconds to 1 minute, making sure they don't burn.

5 Crush the spices in a mortar and pestle. Add the ginger and garlic and continue to work to a pulp. Work in the lime or lemon juice.

6 Mix together the peppers, spice mixture, onion and herbs. Season to taste and spoon into a serving bowl. Chill for 1–2 hours before serving as an accompaniment to barbecued meats or Haloumi cheese kebabs.

Mango and Radish Salsa

The sweet flavor and juicy texture of mango in this salsa contrasts very well with the hot and crunchy radishes. Serve with plain grilled fish or chicken.

Serves 4

INGREDIENTS
1 large, ripe mango
12 radishes
juice of 1 lemon
3 tbsp olive oil
red Tabasco sauce, to taste
3 tbsp chopped fresh
    cilantro
1 tsp pink peppercorns
salt

TO SERVE
lettuce leaves
watercress sprigs
slices of sesame or rye bread

mango   radishes

olive oil   lemon juice   red Tabasco sauce

cilantro   pink peppercorns

1 Holding the mango upright on a cutting board, use a large knife to slice the flesh away from either side of the large flat pit in two pieces. Using a smaller knife, carefully trim away any flesh still clinging to the top and bottom of the pit.

2 Score the flesh of the mango halves deeply, taking care to avoid cutting through the skin: make parallel incisions about ½ in apart; turn and cut lines in the opposite direction. Carefully turn the skin inside out so the flesh stands out like porcupine spikes. Slice the diced flesh away from the skin.

3 Trim the radishes, discarding the root tails and leaves. Coarsely grate the radishes or dice them finely and place in a bowl with the mango cubes.

4 Stir the lemon juice and olive oil with salt and a few drops of Tabasco sauce to taste, then stir in the chopped cilantro.

5 Coarsely crush the pink peppercorns in a mortar and pestle or place them on a cutting board and flatten them with the heel of a heavy-bladed knife. Stir into the lemon oil.

6 Toss the radishes and mango, pour in the dressing and toss again. Chill for up to 2 hours before serving.

VARIATION
Try using papaya in place of the mango in this salsa.

Guacamole

Nachos or tortilla chips are the perfect accompaniment for this classic Mexican dip.

Serves 4

INGREDIENTS
2 ripe avocados
2 red chilies, seeded
1 garlic clove
1 shallot
2 tbsp olive oil, plus extra
  to serve
juice of 1 lemon
salt
Italian parsley leaves, to garnish

avocados

red chilies

shallot

olive oil

garlic

Italian parsley

lemon juice

1 Halve the avocados, remove their pits and, using a spoon, scoop out their flesh into a bowl.

2 Mash the flesh well with a potato masher or a large fork.

3 Finely chop the chilies, garlic and shallot, then stir into the mashed avocado with the olive oil and lemon juice. Add salt to taste.

4 Spoon the mixture into a small serving bowl. Drizzle on a little olive oil and scatter with a few Italian parsley leaves. Serve immediately.

VARIATION

Make a completely smooth guacamole by mixing the ingredients in a blender or food processor. For a chunkier version, add a diced tomato or red bell pepper.

Salsa Verde

There are many versions of this classic green salsa. Serve this one with creamy mashed potatoes or drizzled over pan-fried squid.

Serves 4

INGREDIENTS
2–4 green chilies
8 scallions
2 garlic cloves
2 oz salted capers
fresh tarragon sprig
bunch of fresh parsley
grated rind and juice of 1 lime
juice of 1 lemon
6 tbsp olive oil
1 tbsp green Tabasco
  sauce, to taste
black pepper

green chilies

scallions

garlic

tarragon

capers

lime juice and grated lime rind

parsley

lemon juice

olive oil

green Tabasco sauce

VARIATION
If you can find only capers pickled in vinegar, they can be used for this salsa but must be rinsed well in cold water first.

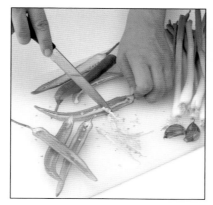

1 Halve the chilies and remove their seeds. Trim the scallions and halve the garlic, then place in a food processor. Pulse the power briefly until all the ingredients are roughly chopped.

2 Use your fingertips to rub the excess salt off the capers but do not rinse them (see Variation, below). Add the capers, tarragon and parsley to the food processor and pulse again until they are very finely chopped.

3 Transfer the mixture to a small bowl. Stir in the lime rind and juice, lemon juice and olive oil. Stir the mixture lightly so the citrus juice and oil do not emulsify.

4 Add green Tabasco and black pepper to taste. Chill until ready to serve but do not prepare more than 8 hours in advance.

Fiery Citrus Salsa

This very unusual salsa makes a great marinade for shellfish and it is also delicious drizzled over barbecued meat.

Serves 4

INGREDIENTS
1 orange
1 green apple
2 fresh red chilies
1 garlic clove
8 fresh mint leaves
juice of 1 lemon
salt and pepper

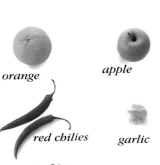

orange   *apple*

red chilies   *garlic*

mint   *lemon juice*

1 Slice the bottom off the orange so that it will stand upright on a cutting board. Using a sharp knife, remove the peel by slicing from the top to the bottom of the orange.

2 Hold the orange in one hand over a bowl. Slice toward the middle of the fruit, to one side of a segment, and then gently twist the knife to ease the segment away from the membrane and out of the orange. Repeat to remove all the segments. Squeeze any juice from the remaining membrane into the bowl.

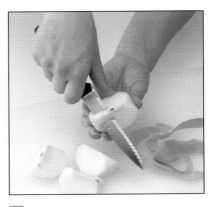

3 Peel the apple, slice it into wedges and remove the core.

4 Halve the chilies and remove their seeds, then place them in a blender or food processor with the orange segments and juice, apple wedges, garlic and fresh mint.

5 Process until smooth. Then, with the motor running, pour in the lemon juice.

6 Season to taste with a little salt and pepper. Pour into a bowl or small pitcher and serve immediately.

VARIATION

If you're feeling really fiery, don't seed the chilies! They will make the salsa particularly hot and zesty.

Cilantro Pesto Salsa

This aromatic salsa is delicious drizzled on fish and chicken, tossed with pasta or used to dress a fresh avocado and tomato salad. To transform it into a dip, mix it with a little mayonnaise or sour cream.

Serves 4

INGREDIENTS
2 oz fresh cilantro leaves
½ oz fresh parsley
2 red chilies
1 garlic clove
⅓ cup shelled pistachios
1 oz Parmesan cheese,
  finely grated
6 tbsp olive oil
juice of 2 limes
salt and pepper

cilantro   *parsley*

garlic   *pistachios*   *red chilies*

olive oil   *Parmesan cheese*   *lime juice*

VARIATION
Any number of different herbs or nuts may be used to make a similar salsa to this one – try a mixture of rosemary and parsley, or add a handful of black olives.

1 Process the fresh cilantro and parsley in a blender or food processor until finely chopped.

2 Halve the chilies lengthwise and remove their seeds. Add to the herbs with the garlic and process until finely chopped.

3 Add the pistachios to the herb mixture and pulse the power until they are roughly chopped. Stir in the Parmesan cheese, olive oil and lime juice.

4 Add salt and pepper, to taste. Spoon the mixture into a serving bowl and cover and chill until ready to serve.

Feta and Olive Salsa

The salty flavor of the feta and olives in this chunky salsa is balanced by the bitter-tasting radicchio.

Serves 4

INGREDIENTS
1 head of radicchio
1 square (9 oz) feta cheese
5 oz black olives, halved and pitted
1 garlic clove
1 red chili, seeded
3 tbsp chopped fresh parsley
2 tbsp olive oil
1 tbsp balsamic vinegar
sea salt

radicchio

feta cheese

black olives

garlic

red chilli

parsley

olive oil

balsamic vinegar

1 Separate the radicchio leaves and rinse them well in cold water. Roughly tear the leaves into small pieces.

2 Cut or break the feta into small cubes. Place the radicchio in a bowl with the feta and olive halves and toss well to combine.

Cook's Tip

Choose unpitted olives such as Kalamata for this salsa – they tend to have a stronger flavor and more interesting texture than the mild, pitted varieties.

3 Finely chop the garlic and chili, and sprinkle them over the salsa with the chopped parsley, olive oil, balsamic vinegar and sea salt to taste.

4 Combine well, then transfer the salsa to a serving bowl and serve at room temperature.

Chunky Cherry Tomato Salsa

Succulent cherry tomatoes and refreshing cucumber form the base of this delicious dill-seasoned salsa.

Serves 4

INGREDIENTS
1 cucumber
1 tsp sea salt
1¼ lb cherry tomatoes
1 garlic clove
1 lemon
3 tbsp chili oil
½ tsp dried chili flakes
2 tbsp chopped fresh dill
salt and pepper

cucumber   *cherry tomatoes*

chili flakes

fresh dill   *chili oil*

lemon   *garlic*

1 Trim the ends off the cucumber and cut it into 1-in lengths, then cut each piece lengthwise into thin slices.

2 Arrange the cucumber slices in a colander and sprinkle them with the sea salt. Set aside for 5 minutes, until the cucumber has wilted.

3 Wash the cucumber slices well under cold water and pat them dry with paper towels.

4 Quarter the cherry tomatoes and place in a bowl with the wilted cucumber. Finely chop the garlic.

5 Grate the lemon rind finely and place in a small pitcher with the juice from the lemon, the chili oil, chili flakes, dill and garlic. Add salt and pepper to taste, and whisk with a fork.

VARIATION
Try flavoring this salsa with other fragrant herbs, such as tarragon, cilantro or even mint.

6 Pour the chili oil dressing over the tomatoes and cucumber and toss well. Let marinate at room temperature for at least 2 hours before serving.

Double Chili Salsa

This is a scorchingly hot salsa for only the very brave! Spread it sparingly onto cooked meats and burgers.

Serves 4–6

INGREDIENTS
6 habanero chilies or Scotch
   bonnets
2 ripe tomatoes
4 standard green jalapeño chilies
2 tbsp chopped fresh parsley
2 tbsp olive oil
1 tbsp balsamic or sherry vinegar
salt

habanero chilies

tomatoes

parsley

jalapeño chilies

balsamic or sherry vinegar

olive oil

1 Skewer an habanero or Scotch bonnet chili on a metal fork and hold it in a gas flame for 2–3 minutes, turning the chili until the skin blackens and blisters. Repeat with all the chilies, then set aside.

2 Skewer the tomatoes one at a time and hold in the flame for 1–2 minutes, until the skin splits and wrinkles. Slip off the skins, halve the tomatoes, then use a tsp to scoop out and discard the seeds. Chop the flesh very finely.

3 Use a clean dish towel to rub the skins off the chilies.

4 Try not to touch the chilies with your bare hands: use a fork to hold them and slice them open with a sharp knife. Scrape out and discard the seeds, then finely chop the flesh.

5 Halve the jalapeño chilies, remove their seeds and finely slice them horizontally into tiny strips. Combine both types of chilies, the tomatoes and chopped parsley.

6 Mix the olive oil, vinegar and a little salt, pour over the salsa and cover the dish. Chill for up to 3 days.

VARIATION
Habanero chilies, or Scotch bonnets, are among the hottest fresh chilies available. You may prefer to tone down the heat of this salsa by using a milder variety.

Indonesian Satay Sauce

There are many versions of this tasty peanut sauce. This one is very speedy and tastes delicious drizzled over grilled or barbecued chicken skewers. For parties, spear chunks of chicken with toothpicks and arrange around a bowl of warm sauce.

Serves 4

INGREDIENTS
scant 1 cup coconut cream
¼ cup crunchy peanut butter
1 tsp Worcestershire sauce
red Tabasco sauce, to taste
fresh coconut, to garnish (optional)

coconut cream

peanut butter

Worcestershire sauce

red Tabasco sauce

coconut

COOK'S TIP
Thick coconut milk can be substituted for coconut cream; coconut milk is usually packed in 14-oz cans, but be sure to buy an unsweetened variety for this recipe.

1 Pour the coconut cream into a small saucepan and heat it gently over low heat for about 2 minutes.

2 Add the peanut butter and stir vigorously until it is blended into the coconut cream. Continue to heat until the mixture is warm but not boiling.

3 Add the Worcestershire sauce and a dash of Tabasco to taste. Pour into a serving bowl.

4 Use a vegetable peeler to shave thin strips from a piece of fresh coconut, if using. Scatter the coconut over the sauce and serve immediately.

Avocado and Red Bell Pepper Salsa

This simple salsa is a fire-and-ice mixture of hot chili and cooling avocado. Serve with tortilla and potato chips for dipping.

Serves 4

INGREDIENTS
2 ripe avocados
1 red onion
1 red bell pepper
4 green chilies
2 tbsp chopped fresh
  cilantro
2 tbsp sunflower oil
juice of 1 lemon
salt and pepper

avocados *red onion* *red bell pepper*

green chilies *cilantro*

sunflower oil *lemon juice*

COOK'S TIP
The cut surfaces of avocados discolor very quickly, so if you plan to prepare this salsa in advance, make sure the avocados are coated with fresh lemon juice to help prevent discoloration.

1 Halve and pit the avocados. Scoop out and finely dice the flesh. Finely chop the red onion.

2 Slice the top off the pepper and pull out the central core. Shake out any remaining seeds. Cut the pepper into thin strips and then into dice.

3 Halve the chilies, remove their seeds and finely chop them. Mix the chilies, cilantro, oil, lemon and salt and pepper to taste.

4 Place the avocado, red onion and pepper in a bowl. Pour in the chili and cilantro dressing and toss the mixture well. Serve immediately.

Sweet Bell Pepper Salsa

Roasting peppers enhances their flavor and gives them a soft texture – the perfect preparation for salsas. Serve with poached salmon.

Serves 4

INGREDIENTS
1 red bell pepper
1 yellow bell pepper
1 tsp cumin seeds
1 red chili, seeded
2 tbsp chopped fresh
   cilantro leaves
2 tbsp olive oil
1 tbsp red wine vinegar
salt and pepper

yellow bell pepper

red bell pepper

cumin seeds

red chili

cilantro

olive oil

red wine vinegar

1 Preheat the broiler. Place the peppers on a baking sheet and broil them for 8–10 minutes, turning regularly, until their skins have blackened and are blistered.

2 Place the peppers in a bowl and cover with a clean dish towel. Set aside for 5 minutes so the steam helps to lift the skin away from the flesh.

3 Meanwhile, place the cumin seeds in a small frying pan. Heat gently, stirring, until the seeds start to pop and release their aroma. Remove the pan from the heat, then transfer the seeds to a mortar and crush them lightly with a pestle.

4 When the peppers are cool enough to handle, pierce a hole in the bottom of each and squeeze out all of the juices into a bowl.

5 Peel and core the peppers, discarding the seeds, then process the flesh in a blender or food processor with the chili and cilantro until finely chopped.

6 Stir in the oil, vinegar and cumin with salt and pepper to taste. Serve at room temperature.

COOK'S TIP
Choose red, yellow or orange bell peppers for this salsa as the green variety is less sweet.

Smoky Tomato Salsa

The smoky flavor in this recipe comes from both the bacon and the commercial liquid smoke. Served with sour cream, this salsa makes a great baked potato filler.

Serves 4

INGREDIENTS
1 lb tomatoes
4 strips bacon
1 tbsp vegetable oil
3 tbsp chopped fresh cilantro leaves or parsley
1 garlic clove, finely chopped
1 tbsp liquid smoke
juice of 1 lime
salt and pepper

tomatoes

vegetable oil

cilantro

bacon

garlic

lime juice

liquid smoke

VARIATION
Give this smoky salsa an extra kick by adding a dash of Tabasco or a pinch of dried chili flakes.

1 Skewer the tomatoes on a metal fork and hold them in a gas flame for 1–2 minutes, turning until their skins split and wrinkle. Slip off the skins, halve, scoop out and discard the seeds, then finely dice the tomato flesh.

2 Cut the bacon into small strips. Heat the oil in a frying pan and cook the bacon for 5 minutes, stirring occasionally, until crisp and browned. Remove from the heat and let cool for a few minutes.

3 Mix the tomatoes, bacon, cilantro, garlic, liquid smoke, lime juice and salt and pepper to taste.

4 Transfer to a serving bowl and chill until ready to serve.

Spicy Avocado Salsa

Avocados discolor quickly so make this sauce just before serving. If you do need to keep it for any length of time, cover closely with plastic wrap and chill in the fridge.

Serves 6

INGREDIENTS
2 large ripe avocados
1 small onion, finely chopped
1 garlic clove, crushed
2 tomatoes
juice of half a lemon
1 tbsp olive oil
pinch ground coriander
few drops of Tabasco sauce
salt and pepper
pinch of cayenne pepper

tomatoes

ground coriander

olive oil

onion

Tabasco sauce

lemon

avocados

cayenne pepper

1 Halve the avocados, remove the pit and scoop out the flesh into a large bowl.

2 Using a fork, mash together with the onion and garlic until smooth.

3 Peel the tomatoes (as for Tomato Salsa), remove the seeds and chop finely. Stir into the avocado mixture with the lemon juice and oil.

4 Season to taste with coriander, Tabasco sauce, salt and pepper. Spoon into small bowls and sprinkle with cayenne pepper. Serve with corn chips and crisp vegetables or serve as a sauce with chili and hot tortillas.

Barbecued Corn Salsa

Serve this succulent salsa with smoked meats or a juicy grilled ham steak.

Serves 4

COOK'S TIP
Make this salsa in summer when fresh corn is readily available.

INGREDIENTS
2 ears corn
2 tbsp melted butter
4 tomatoes
6 scallions
1 garlic clove
2 tbsp fresh lemon juice
2 tbsp olive oil
red Tabasco sauce, to taste
salt and pepper

corn

butter

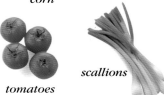

tomatoes

scallions

garlic

lemon juice

olive oil

red Tabasco sauce

1 Remove the husks and silky threads from the corn. Brush the cobs with the melted butter and gently barbecue or grill them for 20–30 minutes, turning occasionally, until tender and tinged brown.

2 To remove the kernels, stand the cob upright on a cutting board and use a large, heavy knife to slice down the length of the cob.

3 Skewer the tomatoes in turn on a metal fork and hold in a gas flame for 1–2 minutes, turning until the skin splits and wrinkles. Slip off the skin and dice the tomato flesh.

4 Finely chop the scallions and garlic, then mix with the corn and tomato in a small bowl.

5 Stir the lemon juice and olive oil together, adding Tabasco, salt and pepper to taste.

6 Pour this over the salsa and stir well. Cover the salsa and let sit at room temperature for 1–2 hours before serving.

Plantain Salsa

Here is a summery salsa, perfect for lazy outdoor eating. Serve with potato chips for dipping.

Serves 4

INGREDIENTS
knob of butter
4 ripe plantains
handful of fresh cilantro plus
    extra, to garnish
2 tbsp olive oil
1 tsp cayenne pepper
salt and black pepper

plantains

butter   cilantro

olive oil

cayenne
pepper

1 Preheat the oven to 400°F. Grease four pieces of foil with the knob of butter.

2 Peel the plantains and place one on each piece of foil. Fold the foil around each tightly to form a package.

3 Bake the plantains for 25 minutes, until tender. Alternatively, the plantains may be cooked in the embers of a charcoal grill.

4 Allow the packages to cool slightly, then remove the plantains, discarding any liquid, and place them in a blender or food processor.

5 Process the plantains with the cilantro until fairly smooth. Stir in the olive oil, cayenne pepper and salt and black pepper to taste.

6 Serve immediately, as the salsa will discolor and over-thicken if left to cool for too long. Garnish with torn cilantro leaves.

COOK'S TIP
Be sure to choose ripe plantains with blackened skins for this recipe, as they will be at their sweetest and most tender.

Yellow Tomato and Orange Bell Pepper Salsa

Serve this sunny salsa with spicy sausages or grilled meats.

Serves 4

INGREDIENTS
4 yellow tomatoes
1 orange bell pepper
4 scallions, plus extra, to garnish
handful of fresh cilantro leaves
juice of 1 lime
salt and pepper

yellow tomatoes

orange bell pepper

scallions

cilantro

lime juice

1 Halve the tomatoes. Scoop out the seeds with a tsp and discard. Finely chop the flesh.

2 Spear the pepper on a metal fork and turn it in a gas flame for 1–2 minutes, until the skin blisters and chars.

3 Peel off and discard the skin. Remove the core and scrape out the seeds. Finely chop the flesh.

4 Finely chop the scallions and cilantro, then mix both with the pepper and tomato flesh.

5 Squeeze on the lime juice and add salt and pepper to taste. Toss well to mix.

6 Transfer the salsa to a bowl and chill until ready to serve. Garnish with shreds of scallion.

VARIATION
Try using a selection of tomatoes, such as plum or cherry, for a variety of textures and flavors.

Fresh Tomato and Tarragon Salsa

Plum tomatoes, garlic, olive oil and balsamic vinegar make for a very Mediterranean salsa – try serving this with grilled lamb chops, or toss it with freshly cooked pasta.

Serves 4

INGREDIENTS
8 plum tomatoes
1 small garlic clove
¼ cup olive oil
1 tbsp balsamic vinegar
2 tbsp chopped fresh tarragon,
  plus extra, to garnish
salt and pepper

plum tomatoes   *garlic*

olive oil   *balsamic vinegar*

tarragon

COOK'S TIP
Be sure to serve this salsa at room temperature, as the tomatoes taste less sweet, and rather acidic, when chilled.

1 Skewer the tomatoes in turn on a metal fork and hold in a gas flame for 1–2 minutes, turning until the skin splits and wrinkles.

2 Slip off the skins and finely chop the tomato flesh.

3 Using a sharp knife, crush or finely chop the garlic.

4 Whisk together the olive oil, balsamic vinegar and plenty of salt and pepper.

5 Finely chop the tarragon and stir it into the olive oil mixture.

6 Mix the tomatoes and garlic in a bowl and pour the tarragon dressing on top. Let infuse for at least 1 hour before serving at room temperature. Garnish with shredded tarragon leaves.

Orange and Chive Salsa

Fresh chives and sweet oranges provide a lively combination of flavors.

Serves 4

INGREDIENTS
2 large oranges
1 beefsteak tomato
bunch of chives
1 garlic clove
2 tbsp olive oil
sea salt

oranges *beefsteak tomato*

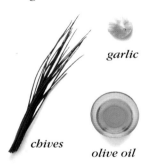

garlic

chives *olive oil*

1 Slice the bottom off the orange so that it will stand upright on a cutting board. Using a large sharp knife, remove the peel by slicing from the top to the bottom of the orange.

2 Hold the orange in one hand over a bowl. Slice toward the middle of the fruit, to one side of a segment, and then gently twist the knife to ease the segment away from the membrane and out of the orange. Repeat to remove all the segments. Squeeze any juice from the remaining membrane. Prepare the second orange in the same way.

3 Roughly chop the orange segments and place them in the bowl with the collected juice.

4 Halve the tomato and use a tsp to scoop the seeds into the bowl. Finely dice the flesh and add to the oranges in the bowl.

5 Hold the bunch of chives neatly together and use a pair of kitchen scissors to snip them into the bowl.

6 Thinly slice the garlic and stir it into the orange mixture. Pour on the olive oil, season with sea salt and stir well to mix. Serve within 2 hours.

VARIATION
Add a little diced mozzarella cheese to make a more substantial salsa.

Aromatic Peach and Cucumber Salsa

Angostura bitters add an unusual and very pleasing flavor to this salsa. Distinctive, sweet-tasting mint complements chicken and other main meat dishes.

Serves 4

INGREDIENTS
2 peaches
1 small cucumber
½ tsp Angostura bitters
1 tbsp olive oil
2 tsp fresh lemon juice
2 tbsp chopped fresh mint
salt and pepper

peaches   *small cucumber*

Angostura bitters   *olive oil*

lemon juice   *mint*

COOK'S TIP
The texture of the peach and the crispness of the cucumber will fade fairly rapidly, so try to prepare this salsa as close to serving time as possible.

1 Using a small sharp knife, carefully score a line right around the circumference of each peach, cutting just through the skin.

2 Bring a large pan of water to a boil. Add the peaches and blanch them for 60 seconds. Drain and briefly refresh in cold water.

3 Peel off and discard the skin. Halve the peaches and remove their pits. Finely dice the flesh and place in a bowl.

4 Cut the ends off the cucumber, then finely dice the flesh and stir it into the peaches.

5 Stir the Angostura bitters, olive oil and lemon juice together and then stir this dressing into the peach mixture.

VARIATION

Use diced mango in place of peach.

6 Stir in the mint with salt and pepper to taste. Chill and serve within 1 hour.

Mango and Red Onion Salsa

A very simple salsa, enlivened by the addition of passion fruit pulp.

Serves 4

INGREDIENTS
1 large ripe mango
1 red onion
2 passion fruit
6 large fresh basil leaves
juice of 1 lime, to taste
sea salt

mango   *red onion*

passion fruit   *basil*

lime juice

1 Holding the mango upright on a cutting board, use a large knife to slice the flesh away from either side of the large flat pit in two portions.

2 Using a smaller knife, trim away any flesh still clinging to the top and bottom of the pit.

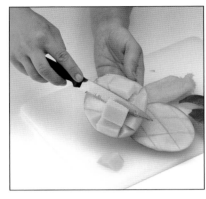

3 Score the flesh of the mango halves deeply, taking care to avoid cutting through the skin. Make parallel incisions about ½ in apart; turn and cut lines in the opposite direction. Carefully turn the skin inside out so the flesh stands out like porcupine spikes. Slice the dice away from the skin.

4 Finely chop the red onion and place it in a bowl with the mango.

5 Halve the passion fruit, scoop out the seeds and pulp, and add to the mango mixture.

6 Tear the basil leaves coarsely and stir them into the salsa with lime juice and a little sea salt to taste. Serve immediately.

VARIATION
Corn kernels are a delicious addition to this salsa.

Caramelized Onion Relish

Slow, gentle cooking reduces the onions to a soft, caramelized relish in this recipe.

Serves 4

INGREDIENTS
3 large onions
¼ cup butter
2 tbsp olive oil
2 tbsp light brown sugar
2 tbsp pickled capers
2 tbsp chopped fresh parsley
salt and pepper

onions

olive oil

brown sugar

butter

parsley

capers

1 Peel the onions and halve them vertically, through the core, then slice them thinly.

2 Heat the butter and oil together in a large saucepan. Add the onions and sugar and cook very gently for 30 minutes over low heat, stirring occasionally, until reduced to a soft rich brown mixture.

3 Roughly chop the capers and stir into the onions. Let cool completely.

4 Stir in the chopped parsley and add salt and pepper to taste. Cover and chill until ready to serve.

VARIATION
Try making this recipe with red onions or shallots for a subtle variation in flavor.

Tart Tomato Relish

The whole lime used in this recipe adds a pleasantly sour taste. Serve with grilled or roast pork or lamb.

Serves 4

INGREDIENTS
2 x 1-in pieces ginger
1 lime
1 lb cherry tomatoes
½ cup dark brown
  sugar
scant ½ cup white
  wine vinegar
1 tsp salt

ginger

cherry tomatoes

brown sugar

white wine vinegar

lime

1 Coarsely chop the ginger. Slice the whole lime thinly, then chop it into small pieces; do not remove the rind.

2 Place the whole tomatoes, sugar, vinegar, salt, ginger and lime together in a saucepan.

3 Bring to a boil, stirring until the sugar dissolves, then simmer rapidly for 45 minutes. Stir regularly until the liquid has evaporated and the relish is thickened and pulpy.

4 Allow the relish to cool for about 5 minutes, then spoon it into clean jars. Cool completely, cover and store in the fridge for up to 1 month.

VARIATION

If preferred, use ordinary tomatoes, roughly chopped, in place of the cherry tomatoes.

Chili Relish

This spicy relish will keep for at least a week in the fridge. Serve it with grilled sausages and burgers.

INGREDIENTS
6 tomatoes
1 onion
1 red bell pepper, seeded
2 garlic cloves
2 tbsp olive oil
1 tsp ground cinnamon
1 tsp dried chili flakes
1 tsp ground ginger
1 tsp salt
½ tsp freshly ground
  black pepper
⅓ cup light brown
  sugar
5 tbsp cider vinegar
handful of fresh basil leaves

tomatoes

onion

garlic   red bell pepper   olive oil

ground
cinnamon   chili flakes

ground
ginger

brown sugar

basil

cider vinegar

COOK'S TIP
This relish thickens slightly as it cools, so do not worry if the mixture seems a little wet at the end of step 5.

1 Skewer each of the tomatoes in turn on a metal fork and hold in a gas flame for 1–2 minutes, turning until the skin splits and wrinkles. Slip off the skins, then roughly chop the tomatoes.

2 Roughly chop the onion, red bell pepper and garlic. Heat the oil in a saucepan. Add the onion, red bell pepper and garlic to the pan.

3 Cook gently for 5–8 minutes, until the pepper is softened. Add the chopped tomatoes, cover and cook for 5 minutes, until the tomatoes release their juices.

4 Stir in the cinnamon, chili flakes, ginger, salt, pepper, sugar and vinegar. Bring gently to a boil, stirring until the sugar dissolves.

5 Simmer, uncovered, for 20 minutes, until the mixture is pulpy. Stir in the basil leaves and check the seasoning.

6 Let cool completely, then transfer to a glass jar or a plastic container with a tightly fitting lid. Store, covered, in the fridge.

Sweet Mango Relish

Stir a spoonful of this relish into soups and stews for added flavor or serve it with a wedge of Cheddar cheese and chunks of crusty bread.

VARIATION
Select alternative spices to suit your own taste; for example, add juniper berries in place of the star anise or try cumin seeds.

Makes 3 cups

INGREDIENTS
2 large mangoes
1 apple
2 shallots
1½-in piece ginger
2 garlic cloves
1 cup small golden raisins
2 star anise
1 tsp ground cinnamon
½ tsp dried chili flakes
½ tsp salt
¾ cup cider vinegar
scant ½ cup light
   brown sugar

mangoes

apple

shallots   ginger

garlic

star
anise

golden raisins   ground
cinnamon

chili flakes   cider
vinegar

brown
sugar

1 Hold the mangoes, one at a time, upright on a cutting board and use a large knife to slice the flesh away from either side of the large flat pit in two portions. Using a smaller knife, carefully trim away any flesh still clinging to the top and bottom of the pit.

2 Score the flesh of the mango halves deeply, taking care to avoid cutting through the skin. Make parallel incisions about ½ in apart; turn and cut lines in the opposite direction. Carefully turn the skin inside out so the flesh stands out like porcupine spikes. Slice the dice away from the skin.

3 Using a sharp knife, peel and roughly chop the apple, shallots, ginger and garlic.

4 Place the mango, apple, shallots, ginger, garlic and raisins in a large pan. Add the spices, salt, vinegar and sugar.

5 Bring to a boil, stirring until the sugar dissolves. Reduce the heat and simmer gently for 45 minutes, stirring occasionally, until the chutney has reduced and thickened.

6 Allow the chutney to cool for about 5 minutes, then transfer it to clean jars. Cool completely, cover and store in the fridge for up to 2 months.

Mayonnaise

Mayonnaise is a simple emulsion made with egg yolks and oil. For consistent results, ensure that both egg yolks and oil are at room temperature before combining – around 70°F. Homemade mayonnaise is made with raw egg yolks and may therefore be considered unsuitable for young children, pregnant mothers, and the elderly.

Makes about 1¹/₂ cups

INGREDIENTS
2 egg yolks
1 tsp French mustard
²/₃ cup extra-virgin olive oil, French or
    Italian
²/₃ cup peanut or sunflower oil
2 tsp white-wine vinegar
salt and pepper

1 Place the egg yolks and mustard in a food processor and blend smoothly.

2 Add the olive oil a little at a time while the processor is running. When the mixture is thick, add the remainder of the oil in a slow steady stream.

3 Add the vinegar and season to taste with salt and pepper.

COOK'S TIP

Should mayonnaise separate during blending, add 2 tbsp boiling water and beat until smooth. Store mayonnaise in the refrigerator for up to 1 week, sealed in a screw-top jar.

Blue Cheese and Chive Dressing

Blue cheese dressings have a strong robust flavor and are well suited to winter salad leaves: escarole, Belgian endive, and radicchio.

Makes about 1³/₄ cups

INGREDIENTS
3 oz blue cheese, Stilton, Bleu
    d'Auvergne, or Gorgonzola
²/₃ cup low-fat plain yogurt
3 tbsp olive oil, preferably Italian
2 tbsp lemon juice
1 tbsp chopped fresh chives
black pepper

1 Remove the rind from the cheese. Place the cheese with a third of the yogurt in a mixing bowl and combine smoothly with a wooden spoon.

2 Add the remainder of the yogurt, the olive oil, and lemon juice.

3 Stir in the chives and season to taste with freshly ground black pepper.

French Dressing

French vinaigrette is the most widely used salad dressing and is appreciated for its simplicity and style. For the best flavor, use the finest extra-virgin olive oil and go easy on the vinegar.

Makes about ¹/₂ cup

INGREDIENTS
¹/₃ cup extra-virgin olive oil, French or
    Italian
1 tbsp white-wine vinegar
1 tsp French mustard
pinch of superfine sugar

1 Place the olive oil and vinegar in a screw-top jar.

2 Add the mustard and sugar.

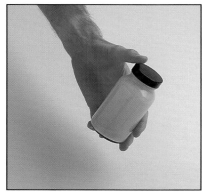

3 Replace the lid and shake well.

French Herb Dressing

The delicate scents of fresh herbs combine especially well in a French dressing. Toss with a simple green salad and serve with good cheese and wine.

Makes about ¹/₂ cup

INGREDIENTS
4 tbsp extra-virgin olive oil, French or
    Italian
2 tbsp peanut or sunflower oil
1 tbsp lemon juice
4 tbsp finely chopped fresh herbs:
    parsley, chives, tarragon, and
    marjoram
pinch of superfine sugar

2 Add the lemon juice, herbs, and sugar.

1 Place the olive and peanut oil in a screw-top jar.

3 Replace the lid and shake well.

COOK'S TIP
Liquid dressings that contain extra-virgin olive oil should be stored at room temperature. Refrigeration can cause them to solidify.

Thai Red Curry Sauce

Serve this with mini spring rolls or spicy Indonesian crackers, or toss it into freshly cooked rice noodles for a delicious main-meal accompaniment.

Serves 4

INGREDIENTS
scant 1 cup coconut cream
2–3 tsp Thai red curry paste
4 scallions, plus extra, to garnish
2 tbsp chopped fresh
  cilantro
1 red chili, seeded and thinly sliced
  into rings
1 tsp soy sauce
juice of 1 lime
sugar, to taste
¼ cup dry-roasted peanuts
salt and pepper

coconut cream

scallions

Thai red curry paste

soy sauce

red chili

cilantro

lime juice

sugar

dry-roasted peanuts

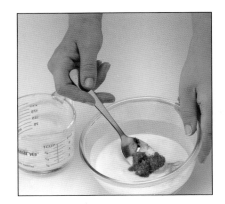

1 Pour the coconut cream into a small bowl and stir in the curry paste.

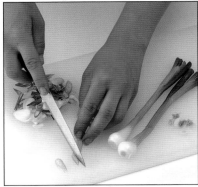

2 Trim and finely slice the scallions diagonally. Stir into the coconut cream with the cilantro and chili.

COOK'S TIP
The dip may be prepared in advance up to the end of step 3. Sprinkle the peanuts on top just before serving.

3 Stir in the soy sauce, lime juice, sugar, salt and pepper to taste. Pour the sauce into a small serving bowl.

4 Finely chop the dry-roasted peanuts and sprinkle them over the sauce. Serve immediately. Garnish with scallions sliced lengthwise.

Melted Cheese Dip

This is a classic fondue in true Swiss style. It should be served with cubes of crusty, day-old bread, but it is also good with chunks of spicy, cured sausage such as chorizo.

Serves 2

INGREDIENTS
1 garlic clove, finely chopped
⅔ cup dry white wine
5 oz Gruyère cheese
1 tsp cornstarch
1 tbsp Kirsch
salt and pepper

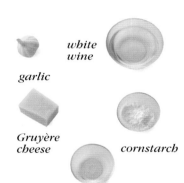

garlic

white wine

Gruyère cheese

cornstarch

Kirsch

1 Place the garlic and wine in a small saucepan and bring gently to a boil. Simmer for 3–4 minutes.

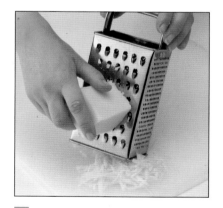

2 Coarsely grate the cheese and stir it into the wine. Continue to stir as the cheese melts.

3 Blend the cornstarch to a smooth paste with the Kirsch and pour into the pan, stirring. Bring to a boil, stirring continuously, until the sauce is smooth and thickened.

4 Add salt and pepper to taste. Serve immediately or, better still, transfer to a fondue pan and place over a spirit burner to keep it hot. Garnish with black pepper.

COOK'S TIP
Gruyère is a tasty cheese that melts incredibly well. Don't substitute other cheeses.

Hummus

This nutritious dip can be served with vegetable crudités or packed into a salad-filled pita, but it is best spread thickly on hot buttered toast.

Serves 4

INGREDIENTS
1 can (14 oz) chick-peas, drained
2 garlic cloves
2 tbsp tahini or smooth peanut butter
¼ cup olive oil
juice of 1 lemon
½ tsp cayenne pepper
1 tbsp sesame seeds
sea salt

garlic

chick-peas

sea salt

olive oil

tahini

lemon juice

cayenne pepper

sesame seeds

COOK'S TIP
Tahini is a thick and oily paste made from sesame seeds. It is available at health-food stores and supermarkets. Tahini is a classic ingredient in this Middle-Eastern dip; peanut butter would not be used in a traditional recipe but it is a convenient substitute.

1 Rinse the chick-peas well and place them in a blender or food processor with the garlic and a good pinch of sea salt. Process until very finely chopped.

2 Add the tahini or peanut butter and process until fairly smooth. With the motor still running, slowly pour in the oil and lemon juice.

3 Stir in the cayenne pepper and add more salt, to taste. If the mixture is too thick, stir in a little cold water. Transfer the purée to a serving bowl.

4 Heat a small non-stick pan and add the sesame seeds. Cook for 2–3 minutes, shaking the pan, until the seeds are golden. Let cool, then sprinkle over the purée.

Cannellini Bean Dip

This soft bean dip or pâté is good spread on wheat crackers or toasted English muffins. Alternatively, it can be served with wedges of tomato and a crisp green salad.

Serves 4

INGREDIENTS
1 can (14 oz) cannellini beans
grated rind and juice of 1 lemon
2 tbsp olive oil
1 garlic clove, finely chopped
2 tbsp chopped fresh parsley
red Tabasco sauce, to taste
cayenne pepper
salt and black pepper

cannellini beans

olive oil

lemon juice and rind

garlic

parsley

red Tabasco sauce

cayenne pepper

1 Drain the beans in a colander and rinse them well under cold water. Transfer to a shallow bowl.

2 Use a potato masher to roughly mash the beans, then stir in the lemon and olive oil.

3 Stir in the chopped garlic and parsley. Add Tabasco sauce and salt and black pepper to taste.

4 Spoon the mixture into a small bowl and dust lightly with cayenne pepper. Chill until ready to serve.

VARIATION
Other beans can be used for this dip – for example, pinto beans or kidney beans.

Chili Bean Dip

This creamy bean dip is best served warm with
triangles of grilled pita bread or a bowl of
crunchy tortilla chips.

Serves 4

INGREDIENTS
2 garlic cloves
1 onion
2 green chilies
2 tbsp vegetable oil
1–2 tsp hot chili powder
1 can (14 oz) kidney beans
3 oz mature Cheddar
  cheese, grated
1 red chili, seeded
salt and pepper

garlic

green
chilies

onion

vegetable
oil

chili
powder

kidney
beans

Cheddar cheese   red chili

1 Finely chop the garlic and onion.
Seed and finely chop the green chilies.

2 Heat the oil in a large sauté pan or
deep frying pan and add the garlic, onion,
green chilies and chili powder. Cook
gently for 5 minutes, stirring regularly,
until the onions are softened and
transparent, but not browned.

3 Drain the kidney beans, reserving
the liquid. Blend all but 2 tbsp of the
beans to a purée in a food processor.

4 Add the puréed beans to the pan
with 2–3 tbsp of the reserved liquid.
Heat gently, stirring to mix well.

5 Stir in the whole beans and the
Cheddar cheese. Cook gently for about
2–3 minutes, stirring until the cheese
melts. Add salt and pepper to taste.

6 Cut the red chili into tiny strips.
Spoon the dip into four individual
serving bowls and scatter the chili strips
on top. Serve warm.

COOK'S TIP
For a dip with a coarser texture,
do not purée the beans. Instead,
mash them with a potato
masher.

Lemon and Coconut Dhal

A warm spicy dish, this can be served either as a dip with poppadums or as a main-meal accompaniment.

VARIATION
Try making this dhal with yellow split peas: they take longer to cook and a little extra water has to be added, but the result is equally tasty.

Serves 8

INGREDIENTS
2-in piece ginger
1 onion
2 garlic cloves
2 small red chilies, seeded
2 tbsp sunflower oil
1 tsp cumin seeds
⅔ cup red lentils
1 cup water
1 tbsp hot curry paste
scant 1 cup coconut cream
juice of 1 lemon
handful of fresh cilantro leaves
¼ cup slivered almonds
salt and pepper

ginger
onion
garlic
cumin seeds
sunflower oil
red chilies
red lentils
curry paste
lemon juice
coconut cream
cilantro
slivered almonds

1 Use a vegetable peeler to peel the ginger and finely chop it with the onion, garlic and chilies.

2 Heat the oil in a large shallow saucepan. Add the ginger, onion, garlic, chilies and cumin seeds. Cook for 5 minutes, until softened but not colored.

3 Stir the lentils, water and curry paste into the pan. Bring to a boil, cover and cook gently over low heat for 15–20 minutes, stirring occasionally, until the lentils are just tender and not yet broken.

4 Stir in all but 2 tbsp of the coconut cream. Bring to a boil and cook, uncovered, for 15–20 more minutes, until the mixture is thick and pulpy. Remove from the heat, then stir in the lemon juice and the whole cilantro leaves. Add salt and pepper to taste.

5 Heat a large frying pan and cook the slivered almonds for 1–2 minutes on each side, until golden brown. Stir about three-quarters of the toasted almonds into the dhal.

6 Transfer the dhal to a serving bowl and swirl in the remaining coconut cream. Scatter the reserved almonds on top and serve warm.

Butternut Squash and Parmesan Dip

Butternut squash has a rich, nutty flavor and tastes especially good roasted. Serve this dip with melba toast or cheese straws.

Serves 4

INGREDIENTS
1 butternut squash
1 tbsp butter
4 garlic cloves, unpeeled
2 tbsp freshly grated
   Parmesan cheese
3–5 tbsp heavy cream
salt and pepper

butternut squash

garlic

butter

Parmesan cheese

heavy cream

COOK'S TIP

If you don't have a blender or food processor, simply mash the squash in a bowl using a potato masher, then beat in the grated cheese and cream using a wooden spoon.

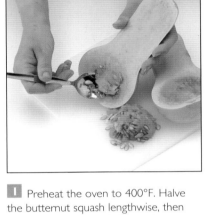

1 Preheat the oven to 400°F. Halve the butternut squash lengthwise, then scoop out and discard the seeds.

2 Use a small, sharp knife to deeply score the flesh in a criss-cross pattern; cut as close to the skin as possible, but take care not to cut through it.

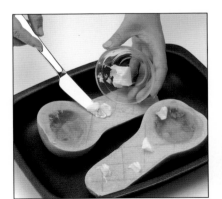

3 Arrange both halves in a small roasting pan and dot them with the butter. Sprinkle with salt and pepper and roast for 20 minutes.

4 Tuck the unpeeled garlic cloves around the squash in the roasting pan and continue baking for 20 minutes, until the squash is tender and softened.

5 Scoop the flesh out of the squash shells and place it in a blender or food processor. Slip the garlic cloves out of their skins and add to the squash. Process until smooth.

VARIATION

Try making this dip with
pumpkin or other types of
squash, such as acorn squash or
New Zealand kabocha.

6 With the motor running, add all but
1 tsp of the Parmesan cheese and then
the cream. Check the seasoning and
spoon the dip into a serving bowl; it is at
its best served warm. Scatter the
reserved cheese over the dip.

Blue Cheese Dip

This dip can be mixed up in next-to-no-time and is delicious served with pears. Add more yogurt to make a great dressing.

Serves 4

INGREDIENTS
5 oz blue cheese, such as
   Stilton or Danish Blue
⅔ cup cream cheese
5 tbsp plain yogurt
salt and pepper

*blue
cheese*

*cream
cheese*

*plain
yogurt*

1 Crumble the blue cheese into a bowl. Using a wooden spoon, beat the cheese to soften it.

2 Add the cream cheese and beat well to blend the two cheeses together.

3 Gradually beat in the plain yogurt, adding enough to give you the consistency you prefer.

4 Season with lots of black pepper and a little salt. Chill until ready to serve.

COOK'S TIP
This is a very thick dip to which you can add a little more plain yogurt, or stir in a little milk, for a softer consistency.

Zesty Tomato Dip

This versatile dip is delicious served with absolutely anything and can be made up to 24 hours in advance.

Serves 4

INGREDIENTS
1 shallot
2 garlic cloves
handful of fresh basil leaves, plus
    extra to garnish
1¼ lb ripe tomatoes
2 tbsp olive oil
2 green chilies
salt and pepper

shallot

garlic

basil

tomatoes

green chilies

olive oil

1 Peel and halve the shallot and garlic cloves. Place in a blender or food processor with the basil leaves, then process the ingredients until they are very finely chopped.

2 Halve the tomatoes and add to the shallot mixture. Pulse the power until the mixture is well blended and the tomatoes are finely chopped.

3 With the motor still running, slowly pour in the olive oil. Add salt and pepper to taste.

4 Halve the chilies lengthwise and remove their seeds. Finely slice them across into tiny strips and stir them into the tomato mixture. Serve at room temperature. Garnish with a few torn basil leaves.

COOK'S TIP

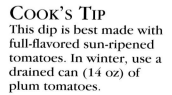

This dip is best made with full-flavored sun-ripened tomatoes. In winter, use a drained can (14 oz) of plum tomatoes.

Mellow Garlic Dip

Two whole heads of garlic may seem like a lot but, once cooked, it becomes sweet and mellow. Serve with crunchy bread sticks and chips.

Serves 4

INGREDIENTS
2 whole garlic heads
1 tbsp olive oil
¼ cup mayonnaise
5 tbsp plain yogurt
1 tsp whole-grain mustard
salt and pepper

garlic

olive oil

mayonnaise

plain yogurt

whole-grain mustard

1 Preheat the oven to 400°F. Separate the garlic cloves and place them in a small roasting pan.

3 Trim off the root end of each roasted garlic clove. Peel the cloves and discard the skins.

2 Pour the olive oil over the garlic cloves and turn them with a spoon to coat them evenly. Roast for 20–30 minutes, until the garlic is tender and softened. Let cool for 5 minutes.

4 Place the roasted garlic on a cutting board and sprinkle with salt. Mash with a fork until puréed.

5 Place the garlic in a small bowl and stir in the mayonnaise, yogurt and whole-grain mustard.

COOK'S TIP

If you are already cooking on a barbecue, leave the garlic heads whole and cook them on the hot grill until tender, then peel and mash.

VARIATION
For a low-fat version of this dip, use reduced-fat mayonnaise and low-fat plain yogurt.

6 Check and adjust the seasoning, then spoon the dip into a bowl. Cover and chill until ready to serve.

Tsatziki

Serve this classic Greek dip with strips of toasted pita bread.

Serves 4

INGREDIENTS
1 small cucumber
4 scallions
1 garlic clove
scant 1 cup plain
    yogurt
3 tbsp chopped fresh mint
fresh mint sprig, to garnish (optional)
salt and pepper

*small
cucumber*

scallions

garlic

*plain
yogurt*

mint

1 Trim the ends from the cucumber, then cut it into ¼-in dice.

2 Trim the scallions and garlic, then chop both very finely.

3 Beat the yogurt until smooth, if necessary, then gently stir in the cucumber, onions, garlic and mint.

4 Transfer the mixture to a serving bowl and add salt and plenty of freshly ground black pepper to taste. Chill until ready to serve and then garnish with a small mint sprig, if desired.

COOK'S TIP
Choose a good quality yogurt for this dip – a thick, rich yogurt will give the dip a deliciously rich, creamy texture.

Sour Cream Cooler

This cooling dip is a perfect accompaniment to hot and spicy Mexican dishes. Alternatively, serve it as a snack with the spiciest tortilla chips you can find.

Serves 2

INGREDIENTS
1 small yellow bell pepper
2 small tomatoes
2 tbsp chopped fresh parsley
⅔ cup sour cream
grated lemon rind, to garnish

yellow bell pepper

tomatoes

parsley

sour cream

lemon rind

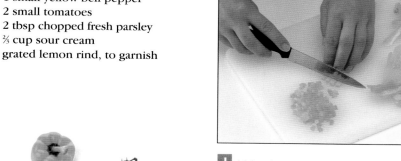

1 Halve the pepper lengthwise. Remove the core and seeds, then cut the flesh into tiny dice.

2 Halve the tomatoes, then scoop out and discard the seeds and cut the flesh into tiny dice.

3 Stir the pepper and tomato dice and the chopped parsley into the sour cream and mix well.

4 Spoon the dip into a small bowl and chill. Garnish with grated lemon rind before serving.

VARIATION
Use finely diced avocado or cucumber in place of the pepper or tomato.

Creamy Eggplant Dip

Spread this velvet-textured dip thickly onto toasted rounds of bread, then top them with slivers of sun-dried tomato to make wonderful, Italian-style crostini.

Serves 4

INGREDIENTS
1 large eggplant
1 small onion
2 garlic cloves
2 tbsp olive oil
¼ cup chopped fresh parsley
5 tbsp crème fraîche
red Tabasco sauce, to taste
juice of 1 lemon, to taste
salt and pepper

eggplant

garlic

onion

olive oil

parsley

crème fraîche

red Tabasco sauce

lemon juice

1 Preheat the broiler. Place the whole eggplant on a baking sheet and broil it for 20–30 minutes, turning occasionally, until the skin is blackened and wrinkled, and the eggplant feels soft when squeezed.

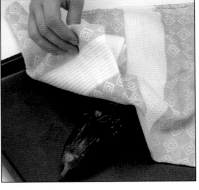

2 Cover the eggplant with a clean dish towel and let cool for about 5 minutes.

3 Finely chop the onion and garlic. Heat the oil in a frying pan and cook the onion and garlic for 5 minutes, until softened but not browned.

4 Peel the skin from the eggplant. Mash the flesh with a large fork or potato masher to make a pulpy purée.

5 Stir in the onion and garlic, parsley and crème fraîche. Add Tabasco, lemon juice and salt and pepper to taste.

6 Transfer the dip to a serving bowl and serve warm, or let cool and serve at room temperature.

COOK'S TIP
The eggplant can be roasted in the oven at 400°F for about 20 minutes, if preferred.

Thousand Island Dip

This variation on the classic Thousand Island dressing is very different from the original version but can be served in the same way – with grilled jumbo shrimp cooked on bamboo skewers for dipping or with a simple mixed seafood salad.

VARIATION
Stir in cayenne pepper or a chopped fresh chili for a more fiery dip.

Serves 4

INGREDIENTS
4 sun-dried tomatoes in oil
4 tomatoes
⅔ cup cream cheese
¼ cup mayonnaise
2 tbsp tomato paste
2 tbsp chopped fresh parsley
grated rind and juice of 1 lemon
red Tabasco sauce, to taste
1 tsp Worcestershire or
  soy sauce
salt and pepper

sun-dried tomatoes in oil

cream cheese

tomatoes

parsley

mayonnaise

tomato paste

Worcestershire sauce

red Tabasco sauce

lemon juice and rind

1 Drain the sun-dried tomatoes on paper towels to remove excess oil, then finely chop them.

2 Skewer each tomato in turn on a metal fork and hold in a gas flame for 1–2 minutes, until the skin wrinkles and splits. Slip off and discard the skins, then halve the tomatoes and scoop out the seeds with a tsp. Finely chop the tomato flesh.

3 Beat the cream cheese, then gradually beat in the mayonnaise and tomato purée.

4 Stir in the chopped parsley and sun-dried tomatoes, then add the chopped tomatoes and their seeds and mix well.

5 Add the lemon rind and juice and Tabasco to taste. Stir in Worcestershire or soy sauce, and salt and pepper.

6 Transfer the dip to a bowl, cover and chill until ready to serve.

Fat-free Saffron Dip

Serve this mild dip with fresh vegetable crudités –
it is particularly good with cauliflower florets.

Serves 4

INGREDIENTS
1 tbsp boiling water
small pinch of saffron strands
scant 1 cup fat-free
  cottage cheese
10 fresh chives
10 fresh basil leaves
salt and pepper

*saffron
strands*

*cottage
cheese*

chives

basil leaves

1 Pour the boiling water into a small
container and add the saffron strands.
Set aside to infuse for 3 minutes.

2 Beat the cottage cheese until
smooth, then stir in the infused saffron
liquid.

3 Use a pair of scissors to snip the
chives into the dip. Tear the basil leaves
into small pieces and stir them in.

4 Add salt and pepper to taste. Serve
immediately.

VARIATION
Leave out the saffron and add a
squeeze of lemon or lime juice
instead.

Spiced Carrot Dip

This is a delicious low-fat dip with a sweet and spicy flavor. Serve wheat crackers or spicy tortilla chips as accompaniments for dipping.

VARIATION
Sour cream may be used in place of the plain yogurt to make a richer, creamy dip.

Serves 4

INGREDIENTS
1 onion
3 carrots, plus extra, to garnish
grated rind and juice of 2 oranges
1 tbsp hot curry paste
⅔ cup low-fat plain yogurt
handful of fresh basil leaves
1–2 tbsp fresh lemon juice, to taste
red Tabasco sauce, to taste
salt and pepper

onion

carrots

orange juice and rind

curry paste

basil

lemon juice

low-fat plain yogurt

red Tabasco sauce

1 Finely chop the onion. Peel and grate the carrots. Place the onion, carrots, orange rind and juice and curry paste in a small saucepan. Bring to a boil, cover and simmer for 10 minutes, until tender.

2 Process the mixture in a blender or food processor until smooth. Let cool completely.

3 Stir in the yogurt, then tear the basil leaves into small pieces and stir them into the carrot mixture.

4 Add the lemon juice, Tabasco, salt and pepper to taste. Serve within a few hours at room temperature. Garnish with grated carrot.

Basil and Lemon Mayonnaise

This dip is based on fresh mayonnaise flavored with lemon juice and two types of basil. Serve with salads, baked potatoes or as a delicious dip for French fries.

Serves 4

INGREDIENTS
2 large egg yolks
1 tbsp lemon juice
⅔ cup olive oil
⅔ cup sunflower oil
4 garlic cloves
handful green basil leaves
handful opal basil leaves
salt and pepper

egg yolks

garlic

lemon juice

olive oil

sunflower oil

green basil

opal basil

COOK'S TIP
Make sure all the ingredients are at room temperature before you start to help prevent the mixture from curdling.

1 Place the egg yolks and lemon juice in a blender or food processor and process them briefly until lightly blended.

2 In a pitcher, stir together both oils. With the machine running, pour in the oil very slowly, a little at a time.

3 Once half of the oil has been added, the remaining oil can be incorporated more quickly. Continue processing to form a thick, creamy mayonnaise.

4 Peel and crush the garlic cloves. Alternatively, place them on a cutting board and sprinkle with salt, then flatten them with the heel of a heavy-bladed knife and chop the flesh. Flatten the garlic again to make a coarse purée.

5 Tear both types of basil into small pieces and stir into the mayonnaise with the crushed garlic.

6 Add salt and pepper to taste, then transfer the dip to a serving dish. Cover and chill until ready to serve.

Curry Mayonnaise with Prawn and Tomato Salad

Curry spices add an unexpected twist to this dressing. Warm flavors combine especially well with sweet prawns and grated apple.

Serves 4

INGREDIENTS
1 ripe tomato
½ iceberg lettuce, shredded
1 small onion
1 small bunch fresh cilantro
1 tbsp lemon juice
salt
1 lb cooked peeled shrimp
1 apple, peeled

DRESSING
5 tbsp mayonnaise
1 tsp mild curry paste
1 tbsp tomato ketchup

TO DECORATE
8 whole shrimp
8 lemon wedges
4 sprigs fresh cilantro

1 To peel the tomato, pierce the skin with a knife and immerse in boiling water for 20 seconds. Drain and cool under running water. Peel off the skin. Halve the tomato, push the seeds out with your thumb, and discard them. Cut the flesh into a large dice.

2 Finely shred the lettuce, onion, and cilantro. Add the tomato, toss with lemon juice, and season with salt.

3 To make the dressing, combine the mayonnaise, curry paste, and tomato ketchup in a small bowl. Add 2 tbsp water to thin the dressing and season to taste with salt.

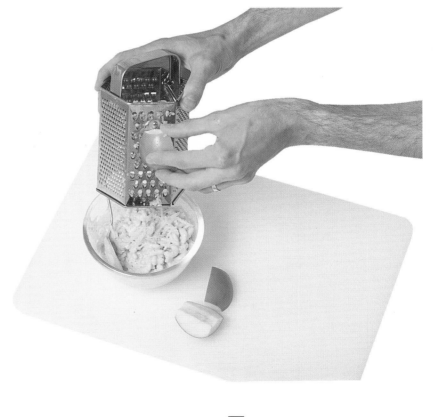

4 Combine the shrimp with the dressing. Quarter and core the apple, and grate into the mixture.

tomato   *apple*

cilantro

lemon

onion

shrimp

COOK'S TIP

Fresh cilantro is inclined to wilt if kept out of water. Keep it in a jar of water in the refrigerator covered with a plastic bag and it will stay fresh for several days.

5 Distribute the shredded lettuce mixture between 4 plates or bowls. Pile the shrimp mixture in the center of each and decorate with 2 whole shrimp, 2 lemon wedges, and a sprig of cilantro.

Fresh Mango Dressing with Grilled Fish

Combining the flavor of mango with hot chili, ginger and lime, this rich, tangy dressing is perfect for outdoor summer meals.

Serves 4

INGREDIENTS
1 French bread
4 redfish, black bream or porgy, each
   weighing about 10 oz
1 tbsp vegetable oil
1 mango
½ in fresh ginger
1 fresh red chili, seeded and finely
   chopped
2 tbsp lime juice
2 tbsp chopped fresh cilantro
6 oz young spinach
5 oz bok choy
6 oz cherry tomatoes, halved

spinach

cilantro

ginger

porgy

cherry tomatoes

mango

1 Preheat the oven to 350°F. Cut the French bread into 8 in lengths. Slice lengthwise, then cut into thick fingers. Place the bread on a baking sheet and dry in the oven for 15 minutes. Preheat the broiler or light the barbecue and allow the embers to settle. Score the fish deeply on both sides and moisten with oil. Broil or barbecue for about 6 minutes, turning once.

2 Place one half of the mango flesh in a food processor. Peel the ginger, grate finely, then add with the chili, lime juice, and cilantro. Process until smooth. Adjust to a pouring consistency with 2–3 tbsp water if necessary.

3 Wash the salad leaves and spin dry, then distribute them between 4 plates. Place the fish over the leaves. Spoon on the mango dressing and finish with slices of mango and tomato halves. Serve with fingers of crispy French bread.

COOK'S TIP
Other varieties of fish suitable for this salad include salmon, monkfish, tuna, sea bass, and halibut.

Egg and Lemon Mayonnaise

This recipe draws on the contrasting flavors of egg and lemon, with the chopped parsley providing a fresh finish – perfect for potato salad. Serve with an assortment of cold meats or fish for a simple, tasty meal.

Serves 4

INGREDIENTS
2 lb new potatoes, scrubbed or
  scraped
salt and pepper
1 medium onion, finely chopped
1 egg, hard-cooked
1¼ cups mayonnaise
1 clove garlic, crushed
finely grated zest and juice of 1 lemon
4 tbsp chopped fresh parsley

COOK'S TIP
At certain times of the year potatoes are inclined to fall apart when boiled. This usually coincides with the end of a particular season when potatoes become starchy. Early-season varieties are therefore best for making salads.

egg

garlic

onion

lemon

new potatoes

1 Bring the potatoes to a boil in a saucepan of salted water. Simmer for 20 minutes. Drain and allow to cool. Cut the potatoes into large dice, season well, and combine with the onion.

2 Shell the hard-cooked egg and grate into a mixing bowl, then add the mayonnaise. Combine the garlic and lemon zest and juice in a small bowl and stir into the mayonnaise.

3 Fold in the chopped parsley, mix thoroughly into the potatoes, and serve.

Crème Anglais

Here is the classic English custard; it's light and creamy without any of the harsh flavors or color of its poorer package relations. Serve hot or cold.

Serves 4

INGREDIENTS
1 vanilla pod
1⁷/₈ cups milk
3 tbsp superfine sugar
4 egg yolks

vanilla pod

milk

eggs

superfine sugar

1 Split the vanilla pod and place in a saucepan with the milk. Bring slowly to a boil. Remove from the heat, then cover and steep for 10 minutes before removing the pod.

2 Beat together the sugar and egg yolk until thick, light and creamy.

3 Slowly pour the warm milk onto the egg mixture, stirring constantly.

4 Transfer to the top of a double boiler or place the bowl over a saucepan of hot water. Stir constantly over a low heat for 10 minutes or until the mixture coats the back of the spoon. Remove from the heat immediately as curdling will occur if the custard is allowed to simmer.

5 Strain the custard into a pitcher if serving hot or, if serving cold, strain into a bowl and cover the surface with buttered paper or plastic wrap.

VARIATION
Steep a few strips of thinly pared lemon or orange rind with the milk, instead of the vanilla pod.

COOK'S TIP
To help prevent curdling, blend 1 tsp of cornstarch with the egg yolks and sugar.

Chocolate Fudge Sauce

A real treat if you're not counting calories. Fabulous served with scoops of vanilla ice-cream.

Serves 6

INGREDIENTS
²/₃ cup heavy cream
4 tbsp butter
¹/₄ cup vanilla sugar
6 oz semisweet chocolate
2 tbsp brandy

VARIATIONS

White Chocolate and Orange
Sauce:
3 tbsp superfine sugar, to replace
   vanilla sugar
6 oz white chocolate, to replace
   semisweet chocolate
2 tbsp orange liqueur, to replace
   brandy
finely grated rind of 1 orange

Coffee Chocolate Fudge:
¹/₄ cup light brown sugar, to
   replace vanilla sugar
2 tbsp coffee liqueur or dark rum,
   to replace brandy
1 tbsp coffee extract

vanilla sugar

brandy

semisweet chocolate

butter

heavy cream

COOK'S TIP
To make vanilla sugar, break a vanilla bean into several pieces and bury in sugar in a glass jar. Cover tightly and let stand for 24 hours before using.

1 Heat the cream with the butter and sugar in the top of a double boiler or in a bowl over a saucepan of hot water. Stir until smooth, then cool slightly.

2 Break the chocolate into the cream. Stir until it is melted and thoroughly combined.

3 Stir in the brandy a little at a time, then cool to room temperature.

4 For the White Chocolate and Orange Sauce, heat the cream and butter with the sugar and orange rind in the top of a double boiler, until dissolved. Then, follow the recipe to the end, but using white chocolate and orange liqueur instead.

5 For the Coffee Chocolate Fudge, follow the recipe, using light brown sugar and coffee liqueur or rum. Stir in the coffee extract at the end.

6 Serve the sauce over cream-filled profiteroles, and serve any that is left over separately.

Ginger and Honey Syrup

Especially good for winter desserts, this sauce can be served hot or cold.

Serves 4

INGREDIENTS
1 lemon
4 green cardamom pods
1 cinnamon stick
²/₃ cup honey
2 tbsp ginger syrup, from the jar
3 pieces crystallized ginger

green cardamom pods

cinnamon stick

lemon

honey

crystallized ginger

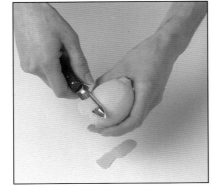

1 Thinly pare 2 strips of rind from the lemon with a potato peeler.

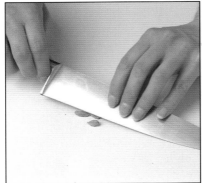

2 Lightly crush the cardamom pods with the back of a heavy-bladed knife.

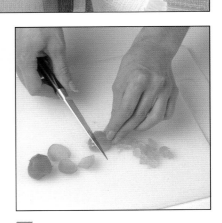

3 Place the lemon rind, cardamom, cinnamon stick, honey and ginger syrup in a heavy-bottomed saucepan with 60 ml/4 tbsp water. Bring to the boil and simmer for 2 minutes.

4 Chop the ginger and stir into the sauce with the juice of half the lemon. Pour over a winter fruit salad of poached dried fruits and sliced oranges. Chill to serve.

VARIATION

To serve hot with steamed puddings, strain at the end of step 3 before stirring in the ginger and lemon.

Sabayon

Serve this frothy sauce hot over steamed desserts or chill as shown and serve just as it is with light dessert biscuits or whatever you prefer. Never let it stand, as it will collapse.

Serves 4-6

INGREDIENTS
1 egg
2 egg yolks
²/₃ cup superfine sugar
1²/₃ cup sweet white wine
finely grated rind and juice of
   1 lemon

lemon

sweet white wine

egg yolks

eggs

superfine sugar

1 Whisk the egg, yolks and sugar until they are pale and thick.

2 Stand the bowl over a saucepan of hot – not boiling – water. Add the wine and lemon juice, a little at a time, whisking vigorously.

3 Continue whisking until the mixture is thick enough to leave a trail. Whisk in the lemon rind. If serving hot serve immediately over dessert or fruit salad.

4 To serve cold, place over a bowl of iced water and whisk until chilled. Pour into small glasses and serve at once.

COOK'S TIP
A generous pinch of arrowroot whisked together with the egg yolks and sugar will prevent the sauce collapsing too quickly.

Butterscotch Sauce

A deliciously sweet sauce which will be loved by adults and children alike! Serve with ice-cream or with pancakes or waffles.

Serves 4-6

INGREDIENTS
1/3 cup butter
3/4 cup dark brown sugar
3/4 cup evaporated milk
1/2 cup hazelnuts

dark brown sugar

evaporated milk

hazelnuts

1 Melt the butter and sugar in a heavy-bottomed pan, bring to a boil and boil for 2 minutes. Cool for 5 minutes.

2 Heat the evaporated milk to just below boiling point, then gradually stir into the sugar mixture. Cook over a low heat for 2 minutes, stirring frequently.

3 Spread the hazelnuts on a baking sheet and toast under a hot broiler.

4 Tip on to a clean dish towel and rub briskly to remove the skins.

5 Chop the nuts coarsely and stir into the sauce. Serve hot, poured over scoops of vanilla ice-cream and warm waffles or pancakes.

VARIATION
Substitute any nut for the hazelnuts, pecans, for example, add a luxurious flavor. You could also add plump, juicy raisins and a dash of rum instead of the nuts.

Red Currant and Raspberry Coulis

A dessert sauce for the height of summer to serve with light meringues and fruit sorbets. Make it especially pretty with a decoration of fresh flowers and leaves.

Serves 6

INGREDIENTS
8 oz red currants
1 lb raspberries
¼ cup confectioner's sugar
1 tbsp cornstarch
juice of 1 orange
2 tbsp heavy cream

orange

confectioner's sugar

heavy cream

cornstarch

red currants and raspberries

1 Strip the red currants from their stalks using a fork. Place in a food processor or blender with the raspberries and sugar, and purée until it is smooth.

2 Press the mixture through a fine strainer into a saucepan and discard the seeds and pulp.

3 Blend the cornstarch with the orange juice, then stir into the fruit purée. Bring to the boil, stirring constantly, and cook for 1–2 minutes until smooth and thick. Leave until cold.

4 Spoon the sauce over each plate. Drip the cream from a teaspoon to make small dots evenly around the edge. Draw a toothpick through the dots to form heart shapes. Scoop or spoon sorbet into the middle and decorate with flowers.

Lemon and Lime Sauce

A tangy, refreshing sauce to end a heavy meal, it goes well with crepes or fruit tarts.

Serves 4

INGREDIENTS
1 lemon
2 limes
1/4 cup superfine sugar
1 1/2 tbsp arrowroot
1 1/4 cups water
lemon balm or mint, to garnish

limes

arrowroot

superfine sugar

lemon

1 Using a citrus zester, peel the rinds thinly from the lemon and limes. Squeeze the juice from the fruit.

2 Place the rind in a pan, cover with water and bring to the boil. Drain through a strainer and reserve the rind.

3 In a small bowl, mix a little sugar with the arrowroot. Blend in enough water to make a smooth paste. Heat the remaining water, pour in the arrowroot, and stir constantly until the sauce boils and thickens.

4 Stir in the remaining sugar, citrus juice and reserved rind, and serve hot with freshly made crepes. Decorate with lemon balm or mint.

VARIATION

This sauce can also be made with orange and lemon rind if you prefer, and makes an ideal accompaniment for a rich orange or mandarin cheesecake.

Brandy Butter

Traditionally served with plum pudding and mince pies, but a good spoonful on a hot baked apple is equally delicious.

Serves 6

INGREDIENTS
1/2 cup butter
1/2 cup confectioner's, superfine or light brown sugar
3 tbsp brandy

butter

light brown sugar

brandy

1 Cream the butter until very pale and soft.

2 Beat in the sugar gradually.

3 Add the brandy, a few drops at a time, beating constantly. Add enough for a good flavor but take care it does not curdle.

4 Spoon into a small serving dish and allow to harden. Alternatively, spread onto aluminium foil and chill until firm. Cut into shapes with small fancy cutters.

VARIATION

Cumberland Rum Butter
Use light brown sugar and rum instead of brandy. Beat in the grated rind of 1 orange and a good pinch of mixed spice with the sugar.

Pineapple and Passion Fruit Salsa

Pile this fruity dessert salsa into brandy snap baskets or meringue nests.

Serves 6

INGREDIENTS
1 small fresh pineapple
2 passion fruit
⅔ cup plain yogurt
2 tbsp light brown sugar

pineapple

passion fruit

plain yogurt

brown sugar

1 Cut off the top and bottom of the pineapple so that it will stand firmly on a cutting board. Using a large sharp knife, slice off the skin.

2 Use a small sharp knife to carefully cut out the eyes.

3 Slice the pineapple and use a small cookie cutter to stamp out the tough core. Finely chop the flesh.

4 Halve the passion fruit and scoop out the seeds and pulp into a bowl.

5 Stir in the chopped pineapple and yogurt. Cover and chill.

6 Stir in the sugar just before serving the salsa.

VARIATION
Lightly whipped heavy cream can be used instead of plain yogurt.

Mixed Melon Salsa

A combination of two very different melons gives this salsa an exciting flavor and texture.

Serves 10

INGREDIENTS
1 small orange-fleshed melon, such
  as cantaloupe
1 large wedge watermelon
2 oranges

cantaloupe

watermelon

oranges

1 Quarter the orange-fleshed melon and remove the seeds.

2 Use a large, sharp knife to cut off the skin. Dice the flesh.

3 Pick out the seeds from the watermelon, then remove the skin. Dice the flesh into small chunks.

4 Use a zester to pare long strips of rind from both oranges.

5 Halve the oranges and squeeze out all their juice.

6 Mix both types of melon and the orange rind and juice. Chill for about 30 minutes and serve.

VARIATION
Other melons can be used for this salsa. For example, try Charentais, Galia or Ogen.

Papaya and Coconut Dip

Sweet and smooth papaya teams up well with rich coconut cream to make a luscious sweet dip.

Serves 6

INGREDIENTS
2 ripe papayas
scant 1 cup crème fraîche
1 piece ginger
fresh coconut, to decorate

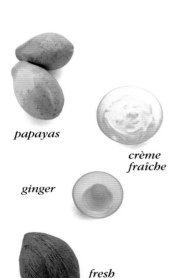

papayas

*crème
fraîche*

ginger

*fresh
coconut*

1 Halve each papaya lengthwise, then scoop out and discard the seeds. Cut a few slices and reserve for decoration.

2 Scoop out the flesh and process it until smooth in a blender or a food processor.

3 Stir in the crème fraîche and process until well blended. Finely chop the ginger and stir it into the mixture, then chill until ready to serve.

4 Pierce a hole in the "eye" of the coconut and drain the liquid, then break open the coconut. Hold it securely in one hand and hit it sharply with a hammer.

5 Remove the shell from a piece of coconut, then snap the coconut into pieces no wider than ¾ in.

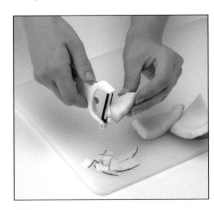

6 Use a swivel-bladed vegetable peeler to shave off ¾-in lengths of coconut. Scatter these over the dip with the reserved papaya before serving.

COOK'S TIP

If fresh coconut is not available, buy shredded coconut and lightly toast in a hot oven until golden.

Raspberry Salad with Mango Custard Sauce

This remarkable salad unites the sharp quality of fresh raspberries with a special custard made from rich fragrant mangoes.

Serves 4

INGREDIENTS
1 large mango
3 egg yolks
2 tbsp superfine sugar
2 tsp cornstarch
scant 1 cup milk
8 sprigs fresh mint

RASPBERRY SAUCE
1 lb 2 oz raspberries
3 tbsp superfine sugar

eggs

mint

mango

raspberries

COOK'S TIP

Mangoes are ripe when they yield to gentle pressure in the hand. Some varieties show a red-gold or yellow flush when they are ready to eat.

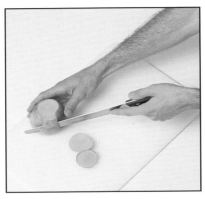

1 To prepare the mango, remove the top and bottom with a serrated knife. Cut away the outer skin, then remove the flesh by cutting either side of the flat central pit. Save one half of the fruit for decoration and roughly chop the remainder.

2 For the custard sauce, combine the egg yolks, sugar, cornstarch and 2 tbsp of the milk smoothly in a bowl.

3 Rinse a small saucepan out with cold water to prevent the milk from catching. Bring the rest of the milk to a boil in the pan, pour it over the ingredients in the bowl, and stir evenly.

4 Strain the mixture back into the saucepan, stir to a simmer, and allow the mixture to thicken.

5 Pour the custard sauce into a food processor, add the chopped mango, and blend until smooth. Allow to cool.

6 To make the raspberry sauce, place 12 oz of the raspberries in a stain-resistant saucepan. Add the sugar, soften over a gentle heat, and simmer for 5 minutes. Force the fruit through a fine nylon strainer to remove the seeds. Allow to cool.

7 Spoon the raspberry sauce and mango custard into 2 pools on 4 plates. Slice the reserved mango and fan out or arrange in a pattern over the raspberry sauce. Scatter fresh raspberries over the mango custard. Decorate with 2 sprigs of mint and serve.

Strawberries with Raspberry and Passion Fruit Sauce

Fragrant strawberries release their finest flavor when moistened with a sauce of fresh raspberries and scented passion fruit.

Serves 4

INGREDIENTS
12 oz raspberries, fresh or frozen
3 tbsp superfine sugar
1 passion fruit
1½ lb small strawberries
8 plain butter cookies, to serve

cookies

passion fruit

raspberries

strawberries

1 Place the raspberries and sugar in a stain-resistant saucepan and soften over a gentle heat to release the juices. Simmer for 5 minutes. Allow to cool.

2 Halve the passion fruit and scoop out the seeds and juice.

3 Transfer the raspberries into a food processor or blender, add the passion fruit, and blend smoothly.

COOK'S TIP
Berry fruits offer their best flavor when served at room temperature.

4 Force the fruit sauce through a fine nylon strainer to remove the seeds.

5 Fold the strawberries into the sauce, then spoon into 4 stemmed glasses. Serve with plain butter cookies.

INDEX

A

ale marinade, winter
   spiced, 84
anchovies:
   anchovy butter, 62
   spicy tuna dip, 69
apples:
   apple sauce, 27
   cider and apple
      cream, 50-1
   fiery citrus salsa, 98
arrowroot, 21
avocados, 9
   avocado and red bell pepper
      salsa, 107
   guacamole, 96
   spicy avocado salsa, 111

B

bacon:
   smoky tomato salsa, 110
bananas, 8
barbecue relish, 126
barbecue sauce, 49
barbecued corn salsa, 112
basil:
   basil and lemon
      mayonnaise, 162
   mango and red onion
      salsa, 124
   pesto sauce, 64
bay, 12
beans:
   cannellini bean dip, 143
   chili bean dip, 144
béchamel sauce, 42
beef:
   Chinese-style marinade
      with toasted sesame
      seeds, 78-9
   winter spiced ale
      marinade, 84
bell peppers, 9
   avocado and red bell pepper
      salsa, 107
   chili relish, 134
   peeling, 23
   roasted bell pepper and
      ginger salsa, 92
   sour cream cooler, 155
   sweet bell pepper and chili
      sauce, 68
   sweet bell pepper salsa, 108
   tomato and roast bell
      pepper salsa, 89
   yellow tomato and orange
      bell pepper salsa, 116
beurre manié, 21

bigarade sauce, 30
bloody Mary relish, 128
blue cheese and chive
   dressing, 138
blue cheese dip, 150
brandy butter, 179
bread sauce, 25
bread sticks, 16
brown sauce, rich, 38-9
brown stock, 18
butter:
   anchovy, 62
   brandy, 179
   garlic, 62
   herb, 62
   herby butter sauce, 44
   lemon and lime, 62
   maître d'hôtel, 62
   mustard, 62
butternut squash and Parmesan
   dip, 148-9
butterscotch sauce, 174

C

cannellini bean dip, 143
capers, 10
   orange and caper sauce, 57
   salsa verde, 97
   spicy tuna dip, 69
   tartare sauce, 35
   tomato and caper salsa, 89
cardamom, 10
carrot dip, spiced, 161
cayenne, 10
cheese:
   blue cheese and chive
      dressing, 138
   blue cheese dip, 150
   butternut squash and
      Parmesan dip, 148-9

cheese sauce, 41
chili bean dip, 144
creamy Gruyère sauce, 73
feta and olive salsa, 101
Gorgonzola and walnut
   sauce, 67
melting cheese dip, 141
pesto sauce, 64
soft cheese and chive
   dip, 14
Thousand Island dip, 158
cheese straws, 16
chervil, 12
chick-peas:
   hummus, 142
chicken:
   spicy yogurt marinade, 82
   stock, 19
chilies, 10
   avocado and red bell pepper
      salsa, 107
   chili and coconut salsa, 90
   chili bean dip, 144
   chili relish, 127, 134
   chunky cherry tomato
      salsa, 102-3
   coriander pesto salsa, 100
   double chili salsa, 104
   fiery citrus salsa, 98
   garlic and chili dip, 60
   lemon and coconut dal, 146
   piquant pineapple
      relish, 129
   preparation, 23
   salsa verde, 97
   sweet bell pepper and chili
      sauce, 68
   sweet bell pepper salsa, 108
   Thai red curry sauce, 140
   tomato salsas, 88

Chinese-style marinade with
   toasted sesame seeds, 78-9
Chinese-style sweet and sour
   sauce, 53
chips, 16
chives, 12
   blue cheese and chive
      dressing, 138
   orange and chive salsa, 120
   soft cheese and chive
      dip, 14
chocolate:
   chocolate fudge sauce, 170
   coffee chocolate fudge
      sauce, 170
   white chocolate and orange
      sauce, 170
cider and apple cream, 50-1
cilantro leaves, 12
   cilantro pesto salsa, 100
cinnamon sticks, 10
clams:
   tomato and clam sauce, 72
cloves, 10
coconut:
   chili and coconut salsa, 90
   papaya and coconut dip, 184
coconut cream:
   Indonesian satay
      sauce, 106
   lemon and coconut
      dal, 146
   Thai red curry sauce, 140
coffee chocolate fudge
   sauce, 170
coriander seeds, 10
corn, 9
   barbecued corn salsa, 112
   corn chips, 16
   spicy corn relish, 131

cornflour, 21
cornichons:
   tartare sauce, 35
coulis, red currant and
   raspberry, 176
cranberry sauce, 28
cream, thickening sauces, 21
crème anglaise, 168
crème fraîche with scallion
   dip, 14
crudités:
   fruit, 16
   vegetable, 16
cucumber, 9
   aromatic peach and
      cucumber salsa, 122-3
   cucumber relish, 127
   preparation, 22
   tzatziki, 154
curries:
   curry mayonnaise, 164-5
   Thai red curry sauce, 140
custard:
   crème anglaise, 168
   raspberry salad with mango
      custard sauce, 186-7

D

dessert sauces, 168-89
dal, lemon and coconut, 146
dill, 12
   creamy dill and mustard
      sauce, 56
dips, 14-15
   basil and lemon
      mayonnaise, 162
   blue cheese, 150
   butternut squash and
      Parmesan, 148-9
   cannellini bean, 143
   chili bean, 144
   creamy black olive, 14
   creamy eggplant, 156
   crème fraîche or sour
      cream with scallion, 14
   fat-free saffron, 160
   garlic and chili, 60
   Greek-style yogurt and
      grainy mustard, 14
   guacamole, 96
   herby mayonnaise, 14
   hummus, 142
   mellow garlic, 152-3
   melting cheese, 141
   papaya and coconut, 184
   passata and horseradish, 14
   pesto, 14
   satay, 54-5

saucy tomato, 151
soft cheese and chive, 14
sour cream cooler, 155
spiced carrot, 161
spiced yogurt, 14
spicy tuna, 69
Thousand Island, 158
tzatziki, 154
yogurt and sun-dried
    tomato, 14
dressings:
    blue cheese and chive, 138
    French, 139
    French herb, 139
    mango, 166

E

eggplant dip, creamy, 146
eggs:
    egg and lemon
        mayonnaise, 167
    sabayon, 173
    spicy tuna dip, 69
    tartare sauce, 35
    thickening sauces, 21
espagnole sauce, 38-9

F

fat-free saffron dip, 160
feta and olive salsa, 101
fish:
    orange and green
        peppercorn
        marinade, 87
    sauces for, 56-63
    stock, 18
fondues:
    melting cheese dip, 141
French dressing, 139
French herb dressing, 139
fruit, 8
    crudités, 16

G

garlic, 10
    garlic and chili dip, 60
    garlic butter, 62
    mellow garlic dip, 152-3
    pesto sauce, 64
ginger, 10
    ginger and honey syrup, 172
    ginger and lime marinade, 81
    roasted bell pepper and
        ginger salsa, 92
golden raisins:
    sweet mango relish, 136
Gorgonzola and walnut
    sauce, 67

Greek-style yogurt and
    grainy mustard
    dip, 14
green peppercorn sauce, 48
guacamole, 96

H

hazelnuts:
    butterscotch sauce, 174
herbs, 12-13
    French herb dressing, 139
    herb butter, 62
    herby butter sauce, 44
    summer herb marinade, 80
hollandaise sauce, 36
honey:
    ginger and honey syrup, 172
horseradish:
    horseradish sauce, 26
    passata and horseradish
        dip, 14
hummus, 142

I

Indonesian satay sauce, 106

J

juniper berries, 10
    red wine and juniper
        marinade, 76

K

kebabs:
    ginger and lime marinade, 81
kidney beans:
    chili bean dip, 144

L

lamb:
    red wine and juniper
        marinade, 76
lemon:
    basil and lemon
        mayonnaise, 162
    egg and lemon
        mayonnaise, 167

lemon and coconut
    dal, 146
lemon and lime butter, 62
lemon and lime sauce, 178
lemon and tarragon sauce, 52
rosemary marinade, 86
lemon grass, 10
lentils:
    lemon and coconut
        dal, 146
lime:
    cilantro pesto salsa, 100
    garlic and chili dip, 60
    ginger and lime
        marinade, 81
    lemon and lime butter, 62
    lemon and lime sauce, 178

M

mace, 10
Madeira sauce, creamy, 40
maître d'hôtel butter, 62
mangoes, 8
    fresh mango dressing, 166
    mango and radish salsa, 94
    mango and red onion
        salsa, 124
    raspberry salad with mango
        custard sauce, 186-7
    sweet mango relish, 136
marinades, 74-87
    Chinese-style marinade
        with toasted sesame
        seeds, 78-9
    ginger and lime, 81
    orange and green
        peppercorn, 87
    red wine and juniper, 76
    rosemary marinade, 86
    spicy yogurt, 82
    summer herb, 80
    winter spiced ale, 84
marjoram, 12
mayonnaise, 138
    basil and lemon, 162
    curry mayonnaise, 164-5
    egg and lemon, 167
    herby, 14
    Thousand Island dip, 158
meat, sauces for, 48-55
melons, 8
    mixed melon salsa, 182
melting cheese dip, 141
mint, 12
    mint sauce, 29
mousseline sauce, 70
mushroom and wine sauce, 34
mustard, 10

creamy dill and mustard
    sauce, 56
Greek-style yogurt
    and grainy mustard
    dip, 14
mustard butter, 62

N

nutmeg, 10

O

olives:
    creamy black olive dip, 14
    feta and olive salsa, 101
    spicy tuna dip, 69
onions, 9
    mango and red onion
        salsa, 124
    red onion raita, 130
    toffee onion relish, 132
oranges, 8
    fiery citrus salsa, 98
    mixed melon salsa, 182
    orange and caper sauce, 57
    orange and chive salsa, 120
    orange and green
        peppercorn marinade, 87
    spiced carrot dip, 161
    tangy orange sauce, 30
    white chocolate and orange
        sauce, 170
oregano, 12

P

papayas, 8
    papaya and coconut dip, 184
paprika, 10
parsley, 12
    cannellini bean dip, 143
    creamy eggplant dip, 156
    maître d'hôtel butter, 62
    parsley sauce, 41
passata and horseradish dip, 14
passionfruit, 8
    mango and red onion
        salsa, 124

pineapple and passionfruit
    salsa, 180
strawberries with raspberry
    and passionfruit
    sauce, 188-9
pasta, sauces for, 64-73
peaches:
    aromatic peach and
        cucumber salsa, 122-3
peanut butter:
    Indonesian satay
        sauce, 106
peanuts:
    satay dip, 54-5
    Thai red curry sauce, 140
peppercorns, 10
    green peppercorn sauce, 48
    orange and green
        peppercorn marinade, 87
pesto:
    cilantro pesto salsa, 100
    pesto dip, 14
    pesto sauce, 64
pine nuts:
    pesto sauce, 64
pineapple, 8
    chili and coconut
        salsa, 90
    pineapple and passionfruit
        salsa, 180
    piquant pineapple
        relish, 129
pistachio nuts:
    cilantro pesto salsa, 100
plantain salsa, 114
potatoes:
    egg and lemon
        mayonnaise, 167
    potato chips, 16
poultry, sauces for, 48-55
pouring sauce, savory, 46

R

radishes:
    mango and radish
        salsa, 94
raita, red onion, 130
raspberries:
    raspberry salad with mango
        custard sauce, 186-7
    red currant and raspberry
        coulis, 176
    strawberries with raspberry
        and passionfruit
        sauce, 188-9
red currants:
    red currant and raspberry
        coulis, 176

spicy red currant
    sauce, 32-3
relishes:
    bloody Mary, 127
    chili, 127, 134
    cucumber, 127
    piquant pineapple, 129
    quick barbecue, 126
    spicy sweetcorn, 131
    sweet mango, 136
    tart tomato, 133
    toffee onion, 132
    tomato, 126
rosemary, 12
    rosemary marinade, 86
roux bases, 20

S

sabayon, 173
saffron, 10
    fat-free saffron dip, 160
    saffron cream, 61
salsas, 88-125
    aromatic peach and
      cucumber, 122-3
    avocado and red bell
      pepper, 107
    barbecued corn, 112
    chili and coconut, 90
    chunky cherry
      tomato, 102-3
    cilantro pesto, 100
    double chili, 104
    feta and olive, 101
    fiery citrus, 98
    fresh tomato and
      tarragon, 118
    mango and radish, 94
    mango and red
      onion, 124
    mixed melon, 182
    orange and chive, 120
    pineapple and
      passionfruit, 180
    plantain, 114
    roasted bell pepper and
      ginger, 92
    salsa verde, 97
    smoky tomato, 110
    spicy avocado salsa, 111
    sweet bell pepper, 108
    tomato, 88
    tomato and caper, 89
    tomato and roast bell
      pepper, 89
    yellow tomato and
      orange bell
      pepper, 116

satay dip, 54-5
satay sauce, Indonesian, 106
sauces, savory:
    apple, 27
    barbecue, 49
    béchamel, 42
    bigarade, 30
    bread, 25
    brown, 38
    cheese, 41
    Chinese-style sweet and
      sour, 53
    cranberry, 28
    dill and mustard, 56
    Gorgonzola and
      walnut, 67
    green peppercorn, 48
    Gruyère, 73
    herby butter, 44
    hollandaise, 36
    horseradish, 26
    Indonesian satay, 106
    keeping warm, 24
    lemon and tarragon, 52
    Madeira, 40
    mint, 29
    mousseline, 70
    mushroom and wine, 34
    orange, 30
    orange and caper, 57
    parsley, 41
    pesto, 64
    red currant, 32-3
    savory pouring, 46
    sweet bell pepper and
      chili, 68
    tartare, 35
    Thai red curry, 140
    thickening, 20-1
    tomato, 66
    tomato and clam, 72
    velouté, 46
    walnut, 71
    white, 41
sauces, sweet:
    butterscotch, 174

chocolate fudge, 170
coffee chocolate fudge, 170
crème anglaise, 168
ginger and honey
    syrup, 172
lemon and lime, 178
red currant and raspberry
    coulis, 176
sabayon, 173
strawberry and
    passionfruit, 188-9
white chocolate and
    orange, 170
savory pouring sauce, 46
scallions:
    barbecued corn salsa, 112
    crème fraîche with scallion
      dip, 14
    salsa verde, 97
    tzatziki, 154
    yellow tomato and
      orange bell pepper
      salsa, 116
serving suggestions, 16-17
sesame seeds:
    Chinese-style marinade
      with toasted sesame
      seeds, 78-9
shallots, 10
shrimp:
    curry mayonnaise, 164-5
    ginger and lime
      marinade, 81
smoky tomato salsa, 110
sour cream:
    sour cream cooler, 155
    sour cream with scallion
      dip, 14
spices, 10-11
squashes:
    butternut squash and
      Parmesan dip, 148-9
stocks, 18-19
    brown, 18
    chicken, 19
    fish, 18
    vegetable, 19
strawberries with raspberry
    and passionfruit
    sauce, 188-9
summer herb marinade, 80
sweet and sour sauce, Chinese-
    style, 53
syrup, ginger and honey, 172

T

tahini:
    hummus, 142

tarragon, 12
    fresh tomato and tarragon
      salsa, 118
    lemon and tarragon
      sauce, 52
tartare sauce, 35
techniques, 18-24
Thai red curry sauce, 140
thickening a sauce, 20-1
Thousand Island dip, 158
thyme, 12
toffee onion relish, 132
tomatoes, 9
    barbecue sauce, 49
    barbecued corn salsa, 112
    bloody Mary relish, 127
    chili relish, 134
    chunky cherry tomato
      salsa, 102-3
    fresh tomato and tarragon
      salsa, 118
    orange and chive
      salsa, 120
    passata and horseradish
      dip, 14
    preparation, 22
    rich tomato sauce, 66
    saucy tomato dip, 151
    smoky tomato salsa, 110
    sour cream cooler, 155
    spicy avocado salsa, 111
    sweet bell pepper and chili
      sauce, 68
    tart tomato relish, 133
    Thousand Island dip, 158
    tomato and caper
      salsa, 89
    tomato and clam
      sauce, 72
    tomato and roast bell
      pepper salsa, 89
    tomato relish, 126
    tomato salsas, 88
    yellow tomato and
      orange bell pepper
      salsa, 116

yogurt and sun-dried
    tomato dip, 14
tortilla chips, 16
tuna dip, spicy, 69
turmeric, 10
tzatziki, 154

V

vanilla, 10
    crème anglaise, 168
vegetables, 9
    crudités, 16
    sauces for, 64-73
    stock, 19
    vegetable crisps, 16
velouté sauce, 46
vodka:
    bloody Mary relish, 127

W

walnuts:
    Gorgonzola and walnut
      sauce, 67
    walnut sauce, 71
warming sauces, 24
watercress cream, 58-9
watermelon:
    mixed melon salsa, 182
white chocolate and orange
    sauce, 170
white sauce, 41
white stock, 19
wine:
    creamy Madeira sauce, 40
    mushroom and wine
      sauce, 34
    red wine and juniper
      marinade, 76
    sabayon, 173
winter spiced ale
    marinade, 84

Y

yogurt:
    blue cheese dip, 150
    Greek-style yogurt and
      grainy mustard dip, 14
    mellow garlic dip, 152-3
    pineapple and passionfruit
      salsa, 180
    red onion raita, 130
    spiced carrot dip, 161
    spiced yogurt dip, 14
    spicy yogurt
      marinade, 82
    tzatziki, 154
    yogurt and sun-dried
      tomato dip, 14